Think And Live:

Challenging Believers to Think

And Thinkers to Believe

Editor: Paul Hughes

Contributors: Lindsay Brooks, Harry Edwards, Paul Hughes, Jeremy Livermore, Mike McCoy, Chris Neiswonger, Richard Park, Steve Tsai

Anderson-Noble Publishing
Las Vegas, Nevada

Visit our Web site at **www.ThinkandLiveBook.com** for more information on this book.

Library of Congress Control Number: 2011901971

ISBN: 978-0-9842827-9-1

Cover design by Ian Maghanoy

Published in the United States of America by:

Anderson – Noble Publishing
An Imprint of Big Guns Marketing, LLC
5348 Vegas Drive, #501
Las Vegas, NV 89108
(800) 551-4376

Contents

Foreword

It's about time the thinkers at Apologetics.com came out with a book. They have been faithfully representing robust Christianity on the airwaves, on the Internet, in churches, at conferences, and on the streets for over a decade. They have a unique story to tell and a lot to teach us, all because they have been committed to engagement, engagement, engagement.

I'm part of a university community in which an individual faculty member spends most of his time teaching his courses and doing his research. On occasion we have a colloquium on campus where we mix it up in terms of ideas with our colleagues and friends. Or, we attend conferences where we present papers and it's not unusual to get feedback or sometimes blowback from the audience. On much rarer occasion we faculty members are invited on to talk radio programs, which is raucous by comparison to the other forums. Compare all of this to what Harry Edwards and his amazing team at Apologetics.com do. They winsomely and attractively make the case for Christ, the Gospel, and the Christian worldview day in and day out in the most hostile environments. Book learning and the non-threatening life of an academic is one thing, but taking your bright mind, first-rank education, and winsome ways out into the mean streets of atheism, religious pluralism, skepticism, naturalism, and so on, is another thing all together.

So there is much to be learned from the years of experience on the front lines of thoughtful Christian interaction with a world gone mad — and this is what the Apologetics.com crew brings to the table. Of course one could read their blogs, follow the arguments on dialogue boards, attend their conferences, or tune in to their radio program. But to have it distilled into a unique book is a dream — especially for us bibliophiles. But this is not the latest stuffy treatise on Christian philosophy and apologetics. Reading *Think and Live* is like sitting down for a frentic conversation with some of the smartest people you know. Sometimes it feels like raw stream of consciousness, sometimes it reads like the first draft of a philosophical or historical monograph. But some how it all comes together every time. They have done some very interesting work turning fast-paced radio programs into a readable text that is a real page-turner.

There are little theological and philosophical gems on every page. So many minds were being poured into the mix that it feels like fields ripe with delicious fruit no matter where you turn. So sit down in a comfortable chair and prepare to have your body relax, while your mind races with amazing ideas that demonstrate the great truths of Christian faith. The Apologetics.Com team can't wait to take you on the ride.

Craig J. Hazen, Ph.D.
Founder and Director
Christian Apologetics Program
Biola University

Introduction

It's amazing to think one of the most influential books in Christianity is *Mere Christianity* by C.S. Lewis — an introductory book on apologetics. I don't know if you knew that. And did you know the content of this famous book was transcribed from his BBC radio shows during World War II? At the risk of sounding pretentious, I note the similarities between Lewis's book and ours. This book is also a transcription of our past radio shows on 99.5 KKLA, in Los Angeles, and yes, written during a war.

I'm not talking about a war like World War II: rather, I believe it's a war of cultures, beliefs, and ideas. In a sense, and some may argue, this war is even more pernicious and devastating than all other wars combined, because in this war the casualties are far too many and the victims suffer eternal consequences.

When the message of the Gospel, the very thing that saves us out of this war, becomes muddled and distorted because of bad ideas, it's time to move. When communicating the solution to the human predicament is compromised because some deny truth, it's time to act. I like what C.S. Lewis himself said:

"If all the world were Christian, it might not matter if all the world were uneducated … [But] to be ignorant and simple now — not to be able to meet the enemies on their own ground — would be to throw down our weapons, and to betray our uneducated brethren who have, under God, no defense but us against the intellectual attacks of the heathen. Good philosophy must exist, if for no other reason, because bad philosophy needs to be answered."

My friends and I are few but we've decided not to retreat in this fight. However, we're also not naive to think that not many will take up the call. That's why we've written this book. We feel this is a book you can read in a weekend. It's simple and clear. Chapters are short but provocative. We also think the title is pretty cool since it helps frame our philosophy of education and ministry: **Belief = Behavior**.

In other words we behave, as we believe. It's not hard to detect our belief when you observe our behavior, and vice versa. For example, in crossing streets, we look both ways, so as not to get hurt; we're careful to not drop fragile objects because we believe in gravity and the item will break; and so on.

This is simplistic, but generally true. In our deepest beliefs, i.e. religion, many remain unchanged or experience less than the "abundant" living. Could it be that our nagging doubts and irreconcilable ideas prevent us from believing the tenets of our faith? At what point do we inspect our duties so it matches well with our doctrine? We're not asking anyone to believe the unbelievable. Nor are we asking you to just behave in certain ways. What we're asking is that you read this book and see if it challenges you to consider truth, and to behave accordingly.

We're asking you to think, and live.

Harry Edwards
Founder & Director
Apologetics.com, Inc.

First ... *Think*

Chapter One: Behold the Man

*It's called **The** Greatest Story Ever Told, which is nearly right. Nearer to the truth is: He is the greatest story ever told. Or as He himself put it: "I AM."*

*Jesus Christ is the single greatest reason to believe. In the end we'll find He's **the only** reason to believe, because all our reasons find their place in Him — as they do from the beginning: "I am the beginning and the end."*

Apologetics begins with Jesus Christ for the quite good and simple reason that everything begins with Jesus Christ.

So we begin with Him: "Behold the Man."

Introduction

Much has been said about Christ. Much can be said about Him. We can never say everything, as the Apostle John saw, long before the last two millennia of spilled ink. The world itself, He told us, would not be able to contain all the books that could be written.

That's what happens when the eternal and temporal meet: we never run out of things to say and do about the collision that results.

Get ready for lots of ink in heaven.

And so we must limit ourselves here and when we talk about our faith. We choose what to say, what not to say, when to say it … and when not to say anything. And we could do a lot worse than talk *only* about Jesus. These limits give power. They're the limits of the gun and the garden hose — narrowing our focus produces incredible energy. It's the kind of energy we see emanating from Jesus, himself, in fact. As with the woman who touched the hem of his robe, and felt His power heal and save, we also draw near and sense that things aren't the same, and that nothing ever will be, not ever again.

Jesus brings it

Into the heat of day and the dark of night, Jesus brings that power, the power of a cool, confident man. His strength can't help producing such results.

In John 3 and 4, he interacts first with Nicodemus at night, then with a Samaritan woman drawing water from a well at midday. They couldn't have been more different: the one is a Jewish man, a teacher, respected and in the know: a leader with power. The other is a half-breed woman, a poor peasant, shunned by her people: what wiles were at one time hers are now waning, and she is on her fifth marriage.

Just prior to this Jesus has been at a wedding, celebrating with friends and family, turning water into wine; he is cryptic in conversation, and direct and good.

So he does water at weddings and water at wells, and talks worship at both. He comments on the geography of approaching God, followed by his impromptu tutoring of a prominent Ph.D. He cares about harvests of souls, and meat to eat that comes directly from God. He considers what it means to be born, and to be born again. He moves from water and wine to the water and the blood. His acts come during celebrations, at work, and when most of us are usually asleep.

Jesus.

He's a real man in real places doing real things. Grass withers and flowers fade, but here we have a man doing stuff we can know and understand ... *Behold the Man*.

People back then saw the crucial question the same way we must now: *who is this guy*? They were entranced and enthralled; they couldn't get enough of him. They crowded him so much that if there had been a fire marshal, He would have shut the whole thing down until they found a room big enough to hold Him.

Maybe next to where we store all those books the world can't contain.

‡

Absent the long and certifying arm of the law, unable to find a large enough room, Jesus preached from boats and hillsides, to handle those crowds. Still they came on and on, tearing the roof off one building, or grabbing his robe; then climbing trees, to see what He would do next, perhaps for them.

Talk about church growth. It got to where the Romans had to put him up on a cross, so the world entire, throughout all history, could see Him, too.

Granted: while he lived and walked among us, some came *solely* to see what he would do next — *do us a trick, God-man ... show us a sign*. Jesus knew that, knew them, knew men's hearts, knew all of everything: what we've never imagined on heaven or earth and in all our philosophy. So sometimes he spoke. As Francis of Assisi might have said Jesus always preached the gospel, and sometimes used words.

But *these* words were truth and life, delivered in distinct ways, as is right and proper from the one who *was* the Word, and Truth and Life, and the Way.

Jesus claims it

What did we think of what he said? Well ... not so much.

We didn't hear it, didn't get it, didn't do it. Still don't.

They didn't have *ears to hear*. But he wasn't always speaking mainly to those around him at the time. He tells us all what to do as only God can — a *command performance* ... every time.

These aren't random statements any more than his acts were senseless. These are new ways to live in the Kingdom of God.

From the Galilean hills (Matthew 4-7) to the Upper Room (John 13-17) He continually says stuff like, "You have heard ... but I say" and "A new commandment I give you."

Who could do that? Easy: no one. There is no Jewish teacher or scribe or prophet who'd try. Try to imagine how appalling this would be to an audience of highly schooled religious men. Sometimes we think, "Golly, Jesus is really special," and that's good as far as it goes. But if we read it in the context, this is not special; it's not even OK. If we're not God, it's punishable by death.

If we're not God.

Who would have the nerve? Not John the Baptist: no prophet, whose line John completed, would think it. Who would dare? Jesus calls himself the light of the world and says, explicitly, *no one* comes to God the Father except through Him. That's not *good teacher* stuff to a first century Jewish hearer. That's blasphemy.

Simply put: **Jesus claimed to be God**. That's the religious reason he's on that Roman cross, visible to all: blasphemy. He claimed to be God, to be the one and only, he with whom we *must* deal to live in the Kingdom. (See box, "Because I Said So.")

When Jesus said this, what happened? How did people respond?

Christ's words get him dead. Like Old Testament prophets stoned for getting it right, Jesus got it right — and got the cross because of it.

Take two examples: one early on and one at the end. In John 8:58, Jesus says, "Surely, truly, I say to you, before Abraham was, *I AM*." Not "I was" but "*I AM*." We know this is huge because in the very next verse they're picking up stones to kill him.

What's the big deal? The big deal is a big word: *tetragrammaton*, the Hebrew designation — it's more than a word — for *Yahweh*.[1] Jesus said he was that God, the one true God, and he knew what he meant — and he knew what it meant to others.

The self-disclosed name is incredible.

You say, "I am" and we wait for you to finish the sentence, to say ... something ... else ... Maybe you are "a student "... or ... "the CEO" ... or "sick as a dog." You and I need to say more if we say, "I am ... " The next word or words give specifics: Are you John, Paul, George, or Ringo?

God goes even farther, by not going as far. He just stops at "I AM." I am? I am what? Well ... I just ... *AM*. God ultimately says I am. Period. That's it.

It's pure essence. It is just ... being.

So here's Jesus. "*I AM*." It's amazing. He's saying, I have always been, always existed, never not existed — *I'm always existing*, which isn't even grammatical, but it is marvelous.

---

[1] The *tetragrammaton* is the unspoken — indeed, unspeakable — name of God. *Yahweh* is the claim of eternal self-existence: his existence depends only on himself: I AM that I AM.

> **Because I Said So** — Matthew ch14-16 (Jesus accepts worship); Mark 14 (Jesus' trial; he says he is God, and he'll judge); John 8 (Before Abraham was, *I AM*); John 10 (I am the good shepherd, cf. Psalm 23: *Yahweh* is my shepherd; I and the Father are one); John 17 (Jesus asks God to glorify Him with the glory they first shared); Acts 14 (Disciples refuse worship) …

You may know Descartes' "I think, so I am" — more precisely, "I am thinking, therefore I am." Well, Christ doesn't even have to think. He just … *AM.*

And they certainly knew *exactly* what he meant. Just two chapters later he says he's one with the Father (John 10:30). In the very next verse they are scuffing around on the ground looking for stones — the really heavy kind — to kill him. Like the prophets of old, this guy Jesus messed up big time. He knew what he was doing. They knew what they were doing.

He knows what he's doing.

Today it can sound like no biggie. Fruitcakes claiming godhood aren't 'zactly unknown. Heck — most of us think we're god, based on how we live and treat others.

It's a big deal. They knew what he was claiming. Jesus was Jewish and he was speaking to Jews. He knew how to say "I am God" in a way they would understand in their cultural context. And he did say it. And they understood it. And they tried to stone him for it.

If he'd said, "I am Jesus" they'd still want to shut him up, as he was causing trouble. What he did say is something else. He used the name of God, the unspeakable name of God … that one, and we know from their reaction what they thought of it.

At the end of his work, he does the same thing again, and it's clear he knows who he is, and what it means — right then and forever.

Jesus is on trial. Sanhedrin or kangaroo court — either way, whoever stayed thought it was legit. Today, as anyone who's faced even a traffic commissioner for a speeding ticket knows: don't back-sass the judge. In the highest law in the land as far as anyone Jewish is concerned — Jesus says the same thing. And once again, all involved know exactly what he means.

Jesus has been seized in Gethsemane, and after the liars have their say, the judge asks Christ, flat out: are you Messiah? If there were ever a time for him to say, "Messiah? What? No way! Are you kidding?" Here it is. It's not what he says.

Saying "I'm Yahweh" might be a tactical error when starting out. Now Jesus repeats the flub in front of the judge, "And," he adds, "You're also gonna see me sitting at the right hand of the Mighty One, and coming on clouds of glory."

He answered the question all right. He's next to God and coming on a cloud: a cloud meant judgment and the prophet Daniel, who prophesied God would return — on a cloud. He's the conquering king, and if you're not terrified yet, now's a good time to start.

It's not what they do. Instead they condemn him to death. High priest, low priest, and all the priests in between know what he means here. The high priest tears his robe. He has influence over others, over the council, and there's about to be a vote on whether Jesus has blasphemed. Raise a hand if you're voting against the boss who just tore his robes.

Is anyone going to say, "Hey, not the robe — let's get more evidence."

No way. The priest asks if there's any need of more testimony (this is a rhetorical question) and Jesus is condemned.

Take these scriptures (and there are dozens more) and put them on the scales. Pile on the prophecies (we'll get to that in the next chapter). Get it contextualized and parsed our and who-is-the-audience and reacted to.

It's the narrow end of the funnel. Pretty soon only one guy fits.

You could throw out all the evidence. That's one option out there.

Or, like Adrian Monk, we have to say of Jesus, "Yeah, he's the guy."

Jesus means it

Do we *want* Jesus to be God? Many would rather he wasn't.

We must ask ourselves frankly, if it fits our desires better to reject him.

Do people want him to be real, to be God, to be ... *Behold the Man*?

Do we?

Why would we even listen to a guy creating such an apparently hard-case, restrictive religion, going beyond the righteousness of scribes and Pharisees saying, "Hey, you don't commit adultery? It's not enough ... I say, don't even harbor lust in your heart."

Seriously. Why go with that?

It's because Jesus lived like no other, ever. He's not just "good teacher" and when someone tried to make him like everyone else, Jesus made yet another connection between himself and God. Way to raise the bar, huh? Indeed, he did raise the bar: "And I, if I be lifted up ... "

Now everyone is looking.

Some avert their eyes, but nobody, strictly speaking, ignores him. It's not possible. First there's that life he lived. Then, turns out nearly all of us want Jesus on our team: the moralists, the social gospel types ... even the atheists sometimes want to say he's not such a bad guy. Everyone claims him, Mormons to Muslims. We've even heard drug addicts say, "He's just enlightened, you know? All the disciples took mushrooms."

So if we want Jesus Christ, why take a watery one? Go for the whole *megillah*. Don't take a bit here or some there.

Face God now. Don't brush him off. Face him. People don't want to — but you? We're saying ... want it. We gotta want it.

It's the second hardest thing in the world to face him and hear, *who do you say that I AM*? The first hardest thing is answering. C.S. Lewis notes that no mere alteration of evil will turn it into good; we must completely reject any of our pet concerns we wish to retain instead of committing all to Christ.

We must ask ourselves, "What in our life at this very moment keeps us from following Christ?" We've got evidence, and we'll lay it out for all in this book. But it's not about evidence; it's about heart. Every apologetic comes down — actually rises up — to Christ. Every barrier is something in our lives we refuse to give up.

There will be changes in our lives if we accept Christ. We think of the changes as rules, as loss of freedom. We think, heck, if it weren't for the rules, everyone would be a Christian.

The truth is we don't have less freedom following Jesus, but more. We who see Christ from the "other side" of deciding, know the dynamism and the excitement of faith. It's the best deal in the world. And if it's the best deal in the world, we must lay down our lives. So we do.

Then we start working it out, trembling — sometimes literally. We see it come alive in us and others — we see we're not alone in it. We start to learn more about God, love neighbors, perceive beauty, and always — it always comes back to Christ.

That's The Greatest Story Ever Told.

He's the greatest apologetic ever.

And people will want that.

People want that.

Chapter Two: Take and Read

That day in the campus lounge a young Jewish college student sat across from a Christian and blurted, "You can't fool me! You're using a trick Bible!"

The verses are real, the man replied, and they point to Christ. Check your copy of the Scriptures, he added, and the student promised he would.

But he didn't, not for several weeks, until guilt at breaking a promise gnawed at him and desire to prove the man wrong fired his enthusiasm. What he found ended both the guilt and the desire.

In his Tanakh² — which he hadn't read since his bar mitzvah — he found every verse, every prediction the man had referenced.

"I'm in trouble," he said to no one. "Jesus is the Messiah."

Introduction
The simple fact of the above — true — story is not one fact, but many: Scripture refers to or elaborates on Jesus as Messiah hundreds of times, including Old Testament prophecies, New Testament confirmation, and extra-biblical sources.

People who didn't know him, people who knew him, and people who hated him or couldn't care less, all are on the same side of this: the Christ will come, fulfill kingly prophecy, claim divinity.

But how do we know it's not all false?

Scripture tells us … but what about Scripture? It must be reliable. We start with Christ and that means fleshing it out a bit — no pun intended. Then OT prophecies, NT accounts, and all those enemies come forward,

---

² The *Tanakh* is a name for the Hebrew canon, formed by the initial letters (T,N,K) of the Hebrew words for its three parts. It's also called the *Miqra*, meaning, *that which is read.*

to say where this man Jesus walked, talked, and where he was discussed some 42 generations earlier, and still is, some two thousand years later.

Out of treasures, things old

Scripture's scrolls foretell and elaborate the life, death, and Resurrection of Jesus Christ in all its world changing big picturing, and all its glorious minutiae and detail.

Where he'll be born, what he'll do, how he'll suffer, why he can atone. God foresaw it and wrote it down.

One-off prophecy or taking them one at a time, we can say: "Random!" But taken together, they all lead to *Jesus of Nazareth, King of the Jews.*

Paradoxically and perversely, similarities between OT prophecies and the realities of Jesus are used against the Christian narrative. People say, "Because these are so alike, they cannot be true — they must be a faked-up interpolation after the fact."

But before getting bogged down in justifying and explaining (and why do *we* have to justify *our* position, first, anyway?) ask any questioner: "If not Jesus … who? Who else even comes close?" Or in reverse: here is the Christ we say fits the part. He lived then, in this way. How do they fit?

We must look at the Old Testament.

It turns out to be the "flip side" of the New.

‡

One of the best arguments for the historicity and accuracy — hence the reliability — of the Old Testament prophecies of Christ, are the Dead Sea Scrolls.[3] These contain, among other material, an entire scroll of the book

---

[3] Discovered in a Palestine cave in 1947, the papyri and fragments contain much of the OT.

of Isaiah 96 percent identical to other copies of it. The four percent comes out in the wash: scribal errors and misspellings. They predated what we previously had by a millennia showing, among other things, the full text of Isaiah existed 100 years before Christ was born. Pretty good.

Now Isaiah was a prophet, and when God calls prophets, they never want to go — not Moses or Jonah, not Isaiah or Jeremiah. They may say they're unworthy, but there's also a little hem-haw going on here: "Um, no thanks. Get somebody else, K?"

They don't want the job. Who does? They're scared, for good reason: prophesy wrong and you die. The job description is clear, give God that much. But job security is a little tenuous, and not only because God may come after you with a big fish.

The people hated prophets, because it's the "ministry of conviction," and the spiritual gift of telling people they're going to hell.

A lot of prophecy is rebuke and who's fond of that? Coming in God's name, telling us go to him, repent, beg forgiveness … they get it wrong and God is not happy (Deut. 18:20, e.g.). And if they get it right they get stoned. Not a position of power; not something people clamor over. You didn't want to be a prophet. That's the Old Testament standard.

To top it off: after calling them, God often told prophets the people wouldn't listen. Jonah hoped they wouldn't, but Isaiah, Moses, and Jeremiah knew it: their messages would be neither heard, nor heeded. And don't forget David in the Psalms: not specifically a prophet, but definitely talking about God, then and for the future. He marveled that the wicked prosper, that men don't listen, that God is not found, when he's spoken so plainly.

Not much has changed, even for we mere Christians. With more than 300 prophesies of Jesus in the Old Testament it's still said, more than once — more than 300 times — "Anyone can claim anything; anyone can claim to be God and have holy books and get a lot of things right."

> ## The 300 — Some Specific Prophecies of Jesus
>
> Genesis 3:15 — Born as all men: of a woman
> Genesis 12:3,7 — Born of Abraham's line
> Genesis 49:10 — Born of the Tribe of Judah
> Deut. 18:18 — Arises from your countrymen
> Psalm 16 — Rise from the dead
> Psalm 22 — Dies with hands and feet pierced
> Psalm 34 — No broken bones
> Psalm 41:9 — Betrayal by a friend
> Isaiah 7:14 — Messiah born of a virgin
> Isaiah 9:6 — He is God
> Isaiah 42:8 — First and the last, and no other
> Jeremiah 23:5-6 — Messiah the Son of David
> Daniel 7:13 — Has authority, receives worship
> Daniel 9:26 — Dies in 33 AD
> Micah 3:1 — Visits a temple
> Micah 5:2 — Born in Bethlehem

Yes, perhaps anyone can, and get *a lot of things* right. But we're talking everything. The true religion will have it all. OT prophecy was all about him, all directed to him. We don't claim a "C" average, or any average. We don't grade ourselves on a curve — and you can be sure no one else will either. This is pass or fail, all or nothing.

Going back a moment to God and his prophets and his people, we hear the Lord say, through Isaiah and the rest, "Why do you worship dead things? Why do you worship snakes and cows — the creature not the creator?" In other words, why do you choose something less than the ultimate? How stupid is that? Well, there's a moral answer to that question, but for our purposes just now, here's the point:

Why worship anything less than a God toward whom everything points? Any prophecy unfulfilled, or even violated, means either "sorry, no prophecy" ... or "sorry, no God." Go for all of it. Settle for nothing less.

‡

One last point about the Old Testament: know that Jesus considered it God's word. He was a good Jewish man, learned the *Tanakh*, and — even more, extolled it every chance he got. Over and over he quotes from it. Again and again he says, "It is written ... " "It is written ... " — 92 times he said this — and he said not the smallest bit of the scriptures would be lost, or even changed. Scripture is unbreakable. He came not to destroy the law but fulfill it. Good enough. What Jesus confirms, we confirm; what he believes, we believe. Would he quote what he didn't trust?

Put scripture on the scales. Prophecies accumulate. Consider contexts, audiences, expectations, reactions. Like the narrow end of a funnel, it gets to where only one man fits. Either we throw out all the evidence or say, with detective Adrian Monk, "Yeah, he's the guy."

... and things new

Sometimes Old Testament prophecies seem to apply vaguely. Language can be ripe and rife with the ambiguous. So as no civil law works unless it's enforced, and no meaning is received unless one understands, so too is prophecy only real, if it is fulfilled.

Cool thing in the New Testament is that even with mediating language — and passing time — there's a real man in a real place doing real things we can know and understand. Old prophecies are fulfilled in the New.

A key here is *context*. What's the context? Yes, first we have to read the Old as if there were no New — that's how Jesus did it, actually — but as we read the New − given by God − we understand even more. How do people then see what he said and did? What did they expect? What did a guy do or not do when the expectations were or were not met, and *why*? Look at moments where Christ gets certain responses from the people or Jewish leaders or his own disciples. How do these passages fit (or not) in with other passages including (but not limited to) in the Old Testament?[4] Who is the audience? Is there more than one? What did Jesus specifically claim of his words?

All of these questions (and trust us, many more) can be relevant. Only then do we think of applying the prophecy − and *never* do we force the passage to fit. It didn't work for Cinderella's sisters and the glass slipper; it won't work for us.

‡

Jesus is the man − *ecce homo* − and the New Testament is as sure of it as He is.

To begin, know that this is first century material. We have the first and the best. Want to know Jesus? Read those who knew him: Dr. Luke, that meticulous physician; the apostles John and Peter; James his brother; and Paul the Saint, converted within days of the death of Stephen. These men wrote the biographies of Jesus, the letters to the churches, the historically rigorous narratives of what this new "cult of Christ"[5] did.

---

[4] Consider Isaiah 52-53 which prophecies him living wisely, rejected by the people, beaten, silent as attacked, crucified with thieves, buried in a rich man's tomb, rising from the dead, raised up and exalted, his punishment bringing our peace, his wounds for our healing ...
[5] That's what it's detractors called it. Oops.

These authors are unanimous — in history, biography, and letter — on the person and work of Jesus Christ. The *ayes* and the eyewitnesses have it.

Begin with the earliest Christian accounts, by Luke, Paul, Peter, John, and a few folks we aren't sure of. Their writings began to be circulated within a generation of Jesus' death, written by 100 A.D. These words were widely dispersed with copies essentially identical. What do they say?

> ## A Little Help Here
>
> Matthew 5 — Jesus says OT won't pass away
>
> John 10 — Says Scripture cannot be broken
>
> Acts — Disciples' focus continually preach Christ
>
> Romans 9 — Paul says Christ is God over all
>
> Colossians — In Christ all God's fullness lives bodily
>
> Hebrews 1 — He is God's glory, exact representation of His being, sustaining all by His word
>
> Revelation 1 — Jesus is Alpha and the Omega, a title for God in the OT
>
> More than 5,000 manuscripts of the New Testament, with originals dating to 125 AD
>
> One name of Jesus, Emmanuel, means God with us — not God's friend or proxy with us: *God* with us.
>
> *Note: a study by Dr. Peter Stoner at Westmont University shows the probability of eight fulfilled prophecies is one in 100 million billion — 1×10^{17}. This is like filling Texas two feet deep with silver dollars, blindfolding someone, and making them find the one marked dollar. Fulfilling 48 of them make it 1×10^{157} — a mathematical impossibility.*
>
> *Just sayin'.*

One big thing they discuss is Jerusalem: that within six weeks of crucifixion — not six centuries, six years, or even six months — and in the same city where Christ was crucified … Pentecost.

Put that in today's terms. Imagine the public execution of a nationally known criminal is not six Sundays in the past, when his former followers start shouting in the streets that he's not dead. At their back are 3,000 adults from a dozen ethnicities; not locals, let's say. *They will not shut up* — not even after one of *them* is also killed, publicly and gruesomely.

A couple the Apologetics.com people work in journalism and public relations, and they assure us that it's the sort of thing that makes news. As an old-school editor might say, "If it bleeds, it leads" … and there is plenty of blood here.

OK, keep the story going. One of the top-dog executioners going after them — say he watched Stephen fall and was on his way to arrest a few more — and now *he* gets into the act: starts saying the Christ has come.

About the same time we start remembering the *life* the guy lived: three years of visibly contending with authorities. And hey, is that his brother, the one who thought he was a loon, now leading the disciples?

And hey, didn't a whole raft of guys hang with the maybe-dead man, including a small cadre with him 24/7 — 26,400 hours in 1,100 days? It might be they know what was what … right? Doesn't seem they would lie, when large stones and foot-long, inch-thick nails are the reward for doing so.

And hey, what about this Jesus himself, the one they say is alive? We are having trouble finding a motive for him lying. Wouldn't he drop the whole thing when *he* faced the nails? OK, if he was nuts. But wait — his life … we remember his life. The miracles. With Johnny Cash we recall: he turned the water into wine.

Then thing get *serious*.

These guys start writing about it.

If we want to know what Paul taught, what Peter said, what John saw, it's all there. The short version is, "If we're not right about this … scram.

Just bag the whole thing, and kill us now." The authorities took most of them up on that last point; we may do well to consider the first one.

In fact, the Bible does our work for us. It comes to us with the counter-arguments. Interesting strategy: the super-cool questions we're going to ask, it already has. The objections we'll raise ... in there before we crack its shiny leather spine. The reasons why not? Evidence of how.

Like the student ignoring his dusty *Tanakh*, we'll get to it ... eventually. Besides, you're just saying that because you guys believe.

No.

We believe because they said it, and we've found them reliable. And now that we believe, there's more to say. But we accept your challenge (one you may not know you've issued) and we'll address your counter-arguments, objections, and reasons, as we move through this book.

Enemies Among Us

Starting with the outsiders and enemies.

They won't lie: they don't like us enough to do so.

Extra-biblical sources, from those uninterested in the Christ question, to the blasphemously opposed to him, have exactly zero reason to cook the books on Christ. In some cases, these people *hate* Jesus.

So if Paul, Peter, John, and James don't currently count for some, we can start here. First century extra-biblical accounts are from ... the first century — so they overlap anyway. Finally, these records tell of Christ. And that's our goal as well.

Well, the long and the short of it is, in reports written by people who're not followers of Christ, have no reason to fake anything, and if they hate, might even have reason to oppose what his disciples were saying ... they say the same thing. Sure, they don't see the why: if we all agreed on that, we wouldn't need this book.

But — crucially — they agree on the facts. There was a man, Jesus, the Christ. They say "so-called" or somesuch, but the point is: they agree the man Jesus *claimed* to be Christ. Doesn't prove it; doesn't disprove it. Does mean Jesus probably said it, and we should look into the matter.

It's like this in those documents on most major elements of Christ's life. So a problem with saying, "Christians made it all up" is that histories by the non-Christians deny this. That's a pretty big problem.

Look at the first century or so after Christ. Ten sources mention Jesus. Ten sources we have. How many mention Tiberius Caesar? Nine, and no one denies he was a real guy. So to begin at the beginning, you don't just throw out a biased New Testament yahoo because he talks about Christ. If you do that, you also dump a century and a half of history. Yeah, right: Tiberius. Sure, buddy ... he existed. Yep. You selling a bridge, too?

So Jesus was there.

What did he do?

Go to Josephus, who writes about Christ performing great feats. Now Josephus was a Jew collaborating with the Romans, writing a history of the time. Jesus was there, too, doing his thing. Josephus doesn't think all that much of the Christ, of course: the great feats aren't miracles of God, but parlor tricks or worse. But he doesn't deny them. He reports them.

Jesus was there, and he did stuff.

Then what happened?

Babylonian Talmud says Yeshua was hanged (crucified) Passover eve. One of the Plinys (we get the younger and older mixed up sometimes) is in on the act. People everywhere think the Christians are whack jobs for following Jesus.

Fine.

But nobody is saying it didn't happen.

We still must show our *version* is correct. Someone (not you, but maybe someone you know) can say these things don't mean what Christians say they mean. We took historical apologetics, and found to our amazement that an author can agree Jesus lived, died, and rose again, and not follow. Still blows us away, sometimes. But we get it. There's still lots of work to do — a task for the Holy Spirit, who changes hearts.

But on this question: do extra-biblical sources give textual support to his existence? Yeah, they do. He lived, and he did what they say he did.

What we do with that is something else.

‡

Just as we don't have to think, we also don't *have* to believe. We don't have to confess, repent, and follow. The Kingdom of God is open; many don't enter.

We can retain our bias against him, against the prophecy and evidence discussed in this chapter. We can deny Christ's words, and those of ones both close to and far from him in the same time he lived. Their testimony unites — yes, he lived and he did these things — but hearts have reasons we know nothing about.

Hard to believe, but we can prefer darkness to light, and the condition of our hearts to what can happen when we follow him. Did He exist?

This chapter looked at the testimony of witnesses. Future chapters will keep trying to remove hindrances to belief, and all of part two will show what should come next. But did he exist?

Recall the last chapter: the first question may be, *Do we want Him to?* If we search the scriptures to see if these things are so, we should continue searching ourselves to see if we'd like it if they were.

Station Break: Josephus

We don't like people who surrender to save their skins rather than die in battle beside their countrymen. Here we're at least a little glad Flavius Josephus did just that in 66 AD, as the Romans crushed another Jewish revolt in Palestine.

Josephus went from quisling to bootlicker in only four years. Returning to Rome with the army that had just leveled Jerusalem and its temple, he found favor with General Titus. And God, who used Balaam's ass, now used Titus' also, and Josephus became a historian.

He was Jewish and did not believe in Christ. As a traitor he had no plans to rock the armada owned by his new rulers. He wanted to be on the right side — not with the rabble-rousers. If he'd wanted **that** *he could have died at Masada, with the heroes, instead of just writing about it. He finished* Antiquity of the Jews *in 93 AD. This is from Book 18, Chapter 3, Section 3:*

> In the time of Pilate there was a wise man called Jesus. His conduct was good and he was known to be virtuous. Many from among the Jews and other nations became his disciples. Pilate condemned him to be crucified, but those who had become his disciples did not abandon his discipleship. They reported that he appeared to them three days

after his crucifixion, that he was alive, and accordingly he was perhaps the Messiah concerning whom the prophets have recounted wonders.

Some perspective. Harry Edwards is founder of Apologetics.com. Let's say we question his integrity, wonder if he's good and honest. His kids say he is, he's a great guy, and so forth. His wife Minerva likes him. OK. All good.

Assuming Harry has an enemy, let's say one of those guys *says it. "I know Harry, he's my enemy, but you know what? He's wise and virtuous and good."*

That's big. It's enemy attestation *and it's huge. Josephus doesn't say Jesus is a fink and rotten so-and-so. He calls him neither charlatan nor fool. No. It's "He worked wonders, lived well, and people believed." Now* that *sounds familiar.*

Chapter Three: Risen Indeed

*From Christ (Chapter One), and people talking about Him (Chapter Two), even the unfriendly ones (Station Break), is Christ **risen**, people talking about Him, and even the unfriendly ones forced to acknowledge empty tombs and the body gone and hundreds of witnesses and changed lives and ...*

We aren't exaggerating, merely noting, to say the Resurrection of Jesus is the most certain event in history, except creation in the first place. This is fortunate since the Resurrection is also, and not coincidentally, the most pivotal event in history.

[As we noted in the last chapter, this doesn't mean people will believe; it just means it happened. And acknowledging it happened, doesn't mean people will believe, period. It just means they're in trouble if they don't.]

We are, in short, more convinced that Jesus Christ lived and died and rose again than that all those other guy lived and died ... period.

Which, when we think about it, is the big difference among them anyway.

Introduction

"If Christ is not raised, your faith is worthless. You are still in your sins. ... If we have hoped in Christ in this life alone, we are of all men most pitied."

That's Saint Paul in 1 Corinthian 15. Just two chapters after the big and famous one on love, the Apostle lays love on the line: if He didn't rise, all of this is a load of nothing.

If the Resurrection didn't happen, don't believe.

Don't go to church. Don't pray or give.

Don't listen to apologetics.com.

Don't keep reading this book.

Don't waste your time.

Tell us what you really mean

That's called *emphasis*.

The Resurrection is Christianity's capstone, and, like our Savior, it's a hill we die on. Our faith stands in the foundation of the God-Man, Jesus Christ. And it falls if the God-Man "be not raised."

We have to start there. Start with, *the Apostle Paul meant it.* See him as a reasonably smart guy, who knew what he wanted to say — what in fact, he *did* say — and could have said differently if it wasn't so big a deal. He knew how to use imagery and story, and does so dozens of times. This is something else. This is concrete: if Christ did not physically rise from the dead, then we're fools — and not the good kind.

A few years ago, the most recent in a litany of "controversial" biblical "finds" drew attention and discussion to Jesus, because maybe we found his bones. One reply — by Christians and non-Christians both — was it didn't matter one way or the other. The former said Jesus was raised "in their hearts" anyway; the latter said our faith doesn't have to depend on fact, in this case finding the actual bones. Neither group cared, and for a similar reason: they weren't concerned if the Resurrection took place.

This isn't Paul's view. He said it matters if Christ rose from the dead, physically. If He didn't, he says, our faith is useless and we should stop being Christians — that is, stop following Christ, a dead guy who never left the tomb. That's what the Apostle Paul meant.

What did God mean?

By the Resurrection of Christ, God meant it, too. He meant we're really and truly reconciled to Him. Christ's coming meant the Kingdom of God was available to all. He showed this by his life and his death — and his

Resurrection. It was the culmination and confirmation of everything else: His advent, His life, His words, and His death.

If Christ wasn't raised, these things were spit. We're following nobody.

Just the facts

OK. Paul meant it. Jesus meant it. We mean it.

That's the claim: Christianity rests on the Resurrection.

So let's *Joe Friday* this thing: let's look at the facts.[6]

We're going to list the four facts most people not locked up agree on. It's a minimalist approach and it doesn't mean we're all holding hands singing, "We agree on these facts." It just means most men and women who've looked at it can assent to the big picture. Hey, maybe we'd find some people, hopefully only a few, who would say you're not reading, right now, this book. But most would say you are. *Those* are the people we're talking about.

So the common ground for the Resurrection of Jesus Christ includes four facts: First, Jesus died on the cross. Second, He was buried in the tomb of Joseph of Arimathea. Third, the women and then the disciples found an empty tomb. Fourth, Jesus appeared later to his followers.

Most historians agree on these four salient facts.

Notice these facts don't require theism. None say, "Jesus rose from the dead and is God." C.S. Lewis in *Mere Christianity* notes often in the early parts of his book that he's not even talking (yet) about theism, let alone

---

[6] Don't just remember and recite facts — these or any others. We want to show you what's so; that's part one of this book. But it's about love (part two of this book) and you can't get that just by reciting stuff you heard somewhere. Keep praying, and remember it's more.

Christianity. He's simply (merely) laying the foundation with concepts we can all support. So these are the bare bones most can start with:

- Death by crucifixion
- Buried in the tomb
- Tomb found empty
- Jesus appeared

Now comes interpretation. People do offer other accounts for the data. But the question is, *what's the best way?* We're going to contend that God raising Jesus from the dead is the best account, the best explanation. But there are others, and we're going to get into those alternate theories now.

As we do, remember this key issue: if we say *God didn't do it*, that God raising Jesus from the dead is *not* the best account … what is? If the four facts are there, how do we get it done without God?

We don't assume theism in this. With chapters one and two, yes, we're building a case. But for just the four facts — *in re The Matter of the Missing Christ*, as the courts might put it — what theory beats it? What account is going to come together as a rational hypothesis, if not this one: *he rose.*

'That's just your theory'

Though most agree we wrote this book and you're reading it, we'd still have lively discussion on if it's any good. In the same way, agreeing on the four facts, we can still discuss them.

Remember how we said in chapter two that the Bible sometimes even testifies against itself? The first two theories to try to cover all four facts are so old we find them cited in scripture.

The first says Jesus' disciples stole the body.

That's not impossible. It's plausible. It could be.

It's inadequate, but not because we say so. There are reasons.

First, the Gospels don't portray a band of disciples willing and able to do any such a thing. Jesus died bloody, ugly, and shamefully. They were hiding. They thought they'd failed. Maybe they were about to run. Peter denied Jesus outright, and by the weekend, didn't feel much like leading a rebellion. Some had just gone back to their previous work.

They thought they'd been wrong. They followed a man who would be king, restore the nation, expel the Romans, and maybe share some of the juice with his close friends. I mean hey, we've earned it, right? Thirty-six months of traipsing around this desert. But he's dead and they're done.

Imagine the morale.

No way the disciples, scared and despondent fisherman about to flee, could subdue Roman warriors, roll away the stone — a stone Pilate put there, with a guard to make sure the disciples *wouldn't* steal the body — and swipe an embalmed and dead phony Christ. No reason to do it, no way they could or would do it in their state. Death for anyone involved. Not a chance.

Next, even if this succeeded, what do you do with the body and why? You have to make up the resurrection story … why? For monetary gain … to feel good about the last three years … to connect the dots … what? What were they going to use a dead body for? Sheesh — where are they going to keep it? How do you become the fearless faithful, proclaiming Christ's Resurrection in all the earth, when you know he's buried in the backyard?

How do you explain this?

One way to explain it is Jesus died, was buried, rose again, met with this band of misfits, and turned them into the bar-none greatest church growth movement ever invented. That's one way to look at it.

An enemy has done this

Another attempt to explain the four facts *sans* God is similar to the first. But this time the disciples didn't steal the body: their enemies did.

The disciples were puny, weak, and sad — but their enemies were in hog heaven! They were powerful and numerous enough to handle the guards and move the stone. The group draws from Jewish opposition, the Romans, a third party, or some combo. The big question is why?

Might not even need the four facts: why would Jesus' enemies, having just crushed His movement, reverse course by making a resurrection lie possible? It's an incentive for insurgency. No Roman or Jew would, and once the enemies who *had* that body started hearing the disciples claim Jesus was alive, they'd say … err, um … no: here's the corpse.

Not only did this *not* happen, but nobody at the time even thought of *faking* it. When Christians started preaching the Resurrection (because Jesus had risen) nobody invented the idea of *pretending* a corpse was Christ, to try and shut them up. No one went to a random tomb for a stand-in, let alone producing the real body from a known tomb.

People make mistakes

The third possible theory to explain the four facts is … *oops*.

It was a mistake. The women went to the tomb, found it empty, but it was the wrong tomb. It wasn't light enough yet, they got confused, etc.

So hey, you Christians — lighten up. They goofed.

Saying it was all a misunderstanding, big or small, misunderstands a great deal. The tomb belonged to Joseph of Arimathea — a known guy. Might've been a politician or a Jewish leader, we're not sure, but people knew him. He's involved in the burial, and can be relied on for finding it in the first place. The women and disciples go too, wrap him in hundreds of pounds of spices, and then … forget? Get lost? Like living in New York City and not knowing who's buried in Grant's Tomb. Everyone — men, women, the guards, and the Son of God — were in the right place.

But keep it going for a moment. In a few days they forget the tomb of their beloved leader — and they find one with used burial clothing in it, folded to the side, and the tomb is empty. If it wasn't Jesus, who did rise

Many Witnesses

"Multiple attestation" sinks many phony ideas of all kinds. In our case, too many people saw Jesus, people who knew Him, had seen him a lot in three years, for the stolen body and the swoon to gain any traction. Disciples know, the professional executioners know — a mother knows. It was Jesus.

from that wrong tomb? The women run all over town and they're wrong … but someone else rose from the dead that weekend?

And where did Peter and John go? The same wrong tomb? Wouldn't they have gone to the right one (the sun's up now) and seen dead Jesus?

Or, if this was the *wrong* tomb, when the disciples start with the "Jesus is alive" malarkey, nobody says, "That's the wrong tomb," then finds the *right* tomb, and produces that body. We stand with Tommy Lee Jones in

"The Fugitive" — if he's fish food, catch me the fish that ate him. If he's in the tomb, get the corpse, and show us and everyone and the world[7].

It didn't happen. If Jesus were (still) dead people who wanted it to be so could've — and would've — gone right to where they'd left the dead guy, and made it known.

They at least would remember where that tomb was.

It is to swoon

Opponents of Christ's Resurrection want it both ways. First they say, "He's dead because he was never alive again after," then it becomes, "He's alive because he never died at all."

Introducing the swoon theory. Swoon theorists want both: Jesus kinda died but not really; he always stayed just a bit alive, but really and really … really seemed dead. Not really, though.

Also called the "apparent death" theory, this one's interesting because we've been assuming (call us crazy) Christ died. But on this view … not so much. He took a lot of abuse, a severe beating, and He was so close to death everyone thought He was, in fact, dead. Erroneously.

Don't judge them, though. They weren't doctors, professionals; they were just uneducated people, didn't know what clinical death was — I mean, it's not like they'd seen people do it — wait, scratch that. But it's not like they could tell, OK. Heck, they thought epileptics were demon-

---

[7] An interesting corollary theory to the wrong tomb is the "replacement" theory: Jesus was freed and someone else crucified in his place. Barabbas is cited since *bar* means 'son of' and *abbas* means 'the father' — thus the 'son of the father' was crucified. Same problems arise in similar forms. If Jesus were alive (indeed, never dead) how'd he get stab wounds in his side and nail holes in his wrists and legs? Who did the women *not* find in the tomb? Where's the body of Barabbas? Where'd Jesus go? How could all of Jerusalem be so dumb? And so on.

possessed. In the case of Christ, they assumed He died, and put Him in the tomb. In a nice, cold tomb he had three days to rest and heal from his wounds. He did and then escaped from the tomb, presenting Himself to the disciples and women as if He had risen.

We're trying not to be snarky, but Lord, it's hard. The main problem is how it's dumber than it assumes people living 2,000 years ago were. Guy might have epilepsy, and the people of the time might not have that term for it — or maybe, you know, he's demon-possessed. Either way, even an early *anno domini* agrarian gal knows healing when she gets it. Man blind 30 years knows he can see, OK? Lazarus was dead as a raccoon coat, and the people could tell. Uneducated doesn't mean dumb. Anyone can do it.

This is another C.S. Lewis term — it's where we read it anyway — and it's called *chronological snobbery*. It means thinking we're so darn smarter, and likely cuter, than people "back then" ... but don't be mad at them — they just can't help it.

‡

OK, here we go. This description not only puts paid to swoon, it also shows what horrible, bloody, ignominious death looked like in 30 A.D. Maybe we'll take *chronological snobbery* down a peg, too.

Start with the body, beaten beyond belief. Swoon asks us to believe the Romans, experts at warfare and what to do with prisoners, didn't torture Jesus properly.

Consider Christ's death. Water and blood means the Roman soldier hit the pericardium, a water-filled sac near the heart, or the spleen. Either is a blood-and-water issue; both mean death.

What made the wound? This isn't an Olympic javelin — light and built for distance. Think heavy and maximum damage. The weapon is 6½ feet long, with an iron shank or head 1-2 feet long, and weighing 12 pounds.

Longer than a man, heavy as a bowling ball, a blade as long as an arm. A soldier learns how to do it right, or you come back and kill him. Christ is unarmed, stationary, beaten, and nailed to a cross.

Gigantic spear wins.

Swoon theory loses.

Nobody lives forever

Finally, let's just say Jesus didn't resurrect at all. Period. Nothing.

The disciples saw what they wanted to see, to believe, which turns out was a hallucination. The disciples and the women saw what they wished for: a human mirage in the deserts of Palestine.

Appearing to 600 people, multiple times, for 40 days.

See, there's no such thing as mass hallucination. When people dream, they don't dream the same things, at the same times, in the same ways, with the same results. No, dreams are distinct. If they're similar, they're not exact; if two or more people marvel at how close their unreal experiences are … they still do not see the same things. Five guys don't wake up one morning, and call each other going, "Whoa, was that a great fishing trip we all just dreamt or what!"

OK, five guys don't call each other, ever.

But neither do they say, "Oh yeah, wow! Same boat, same ocean, same beer, same big fish I caught … wow!" At which point, of course, the four other guys go, "What do you mean big fish *you* caught?"

See?

Second point: to the Jewish mind, *resurrection* means physical. A ghost or phantom makes no sense to Hebrew thought, because there's no such thing. It's not what resurrection means. Maybe those rubes aren't hicks.

Third, if we advocate apparition, how can eat or have wounds, among dozens of aspects of the risen Jesus? It can't do real things: it's not real.

Just Breathe

With crucifixion it's not the long fall, it's the sudden stop. It kills not so much because you've been nailed to a cross, but when Roman soldiers broke your knees, keeping you from hauling your thrashed carcass upward to breathe. It kills by suffocation. Counter to the practice & confirming prophecy, no one broke Jesus' knees.

Finally, if we all have the same dream of a guy who rose from the dead *who didn't actually rise from the dead*, we again go to an un-empty tomb (or go again, for those who found it empty the first time and "lied") to find … the body. The beaten, bloody, spice-encrusted, and really, very dead, un-risen body of an itinerant Jewish rabbi killed the previous Friday by the Roman government.

The bad news on that whole deal is no resurrection.

Good news is we cure the weird mass hallucination.

Chapter Four: Only Logical

Logic is a problem. On one hand it's really important. On another it's hard. On another it takes work. On another … you begin to see the problem.

Complicating matters, some say logic isn't important at all. Faith is more how you live, what you do, and relationship.

Well, both naturally. It's like that a lot.

*Truth is you need both, as we're saying with this book. One thing that means is you **do** need logic. Otherwise, you don't have both.*

Introduction

"In the beginning was the Word, and the Word was with God … " may be the most famous first words in history. Bigger than "Call me Ishmael" or "It was the best of times, it was the worst of times" or "We hold these truths to be self-evident."

Through verse 18, the hard-core logician might say, *argue* even, the Apostle John lays out a vision of the order, the Word, the *logos* … the **logic** of God. John's Gospel *is* known as the most abstract of them …

But *abstraction* isn't necessarily *logic* and this Gospel is also the most *ethereal* of the four Christ chronicles. In fact, some folks say Luke is far more logical in his strict doctoral, first-this-then-that *history*, to get all events exact. This while John spends a full chapter on prayer and four more on feet washing, plus Jesus telling His disciples to above all love each other.

And don't even get us started on John's epistles.

Now *those* are some heavy-duty love letters.

This man is not writing a dissertation.

So there's plenty of room for contention on this matter. Let's see if we can figure it out a little — logic it a bit … in love, of course.

Gang of four

How many Saviors does it take to light up a room?

None. That's not what Saviors do. Saviors light a universe. That takes only one. Good thing, too, because there is only one.

John's preamble is God speaking, Christ revealing: the One True God who is revealing and the One True God being revealed. He is the light, giving light to every man. If anyone's got any light, he's it. It is not the light of a room, nor the light of the sun, nor the light, even, of the universe. It's the light of reason, and understanding, and love.

Now reason, logic, expresses itself in four kinds of statements: four. If you come up with a fifth, that'd be great — Nobel Prize winning great — but actually, factually, there are only four:

- Universal
- Particular
- Quantification
- Qualification

[*Note: no fair saying* Question *because in logic if we have a question, it's one of the four listed above with a question mark at the end.*]

So with those four we can talk about an aspect of a thing or how many we're talking about, and whether it applies to all of them or to just a few.

- "All cherries come from cherry trees"
- "Sometimes I feel like going to the beach"
- "They don't really make good movies anymore"

- "Jesus is the eternal Son of God manifest in human flesh"

Like that. Statements get more or less complex, but everything affirms something. That's just the way it is. String them together, or not, and it's about whether one thing relates to another, and how it does.

This is crucial, because everything from galaxies to girlfriends ends up being about relationship. How does this thing connect or not to another?

Everything has a context, and they interact with each other, or don't.

You are *holding* one *book*. You either are or you aren't. We hope you are.

Maybe *you* and a *chair* have a particular relationship, *sitting*, as you do.

Later *we* meet *friends* for *dinner*. More relationship. It's there ... or not.

The earth, which hours earlier sat in one particular relationship to the sun, will soon enjoy a different perspective, and the moon will be easier to see. Sleep, blessed sleep ... then alarm clocks of the world will unite, changing the relationship.

We never think of it, and that's OK, but the very reality of all of it, even before we say words, is a proposition. We assert the relationships exist.

Gestures and non-verbal items count, too. Me shaking my head *means* something, and so does this:

These also communicate by the four kinds of statements.

Now one reason Christians are sometimes afraid of reason and logic is we feel like we've been getting our brains beat out for 300 years by guys using tricky arguments against us — making words mean stuff we don't.

Before that, Christians dominated in these areas, where for 1,500 years we saw it as not contrary to faith, but an expression of it. From the 1600s, though, and into the last century, Christians backed off, and, being more or less in retreat, were often beaten back when we didn't move at all.

Further fighting *inside* the church in the last century or so brought logic into some, well … doubt. Is God logical? Does the Bible have meaning in any … meaningful way? How do we know?

We're still reeling.

A modest proposal

To guide faith, we must commit to propositional elements of it. Much we want to say about God involves these. As a side benefit it may also keep us from getting our clocks cleaned by every new generation's new crop of non-new Atheists.

Now *propositional* simply means we have a subject, an object, and some link of the two[8].

It's so simple … and so controversial. It's true. Christians argue about whether faith is logical, or needs to be, or can be. We disagree if it's the first thing or the last thing or nothing. If we ditch reason, will that be a problem? Yes. Can we be devoted to logic and remain rotten? Yes. The conflicts take on terms like *rationalism, pietism,* and *fideism.*

Our question for these discussions is *what place logic*?

Logic touches everything, up to and including questions, even denials, of logic. It's not the only thing, and it isn't always most important, but it

---

[8] That middle one is called a *copula*, but don't worry about remembering it. Not a big deal.

is crucial. An ad slogan of some years back said of a company, *"We don't make a lot of the things you use. We make a lot of the things you use better."*

Logic's like that. For instance, here are ideas related to the word, *word*. As in, "In the beginning was the Word" —

Esteem, reckon, proportion, ratio, theory, argument, explanation, law, principle, reason, formula, debate, speech, narrative, sentence, discuss, oracle, deliberation, wisdom … logic.

Or to put it another way, *"Logic isn't the only part of the things we do, but it makes a lot of the things we do better."*

It helps with scripture, for one. If we want to learn things about God, it is crucial. Thinking about God: who He is, how He is, what He does, and so on: this is going to require logic. The Bible talks a lot about God, and it will not hinder us in our pursuit of him.

The idea itself is crazy, but without propositional meaning, we lose the possibility that the Bible says anything, not just to us, but anything at all. Again: it's not all it says, or the only thing, or at any one time the biggest thing. But it is essential.

Surely this is partly why it's so vital to some that truth be ash-heaped: if any connecting with or even approach to God is impossible, they don't have to *do* anything about relationship with him.

‡

So it helps with scripture and leads to connection with God. How?

Words. Before we can communicate — before we can connect with another by what we say and do, we must say and do something. We recall how actions and non-verbals, shaking the head and stop signs, mean things to; they're "words" as well. So it's what we say and do.

Now what we say and do will have a logical range, meaning what it can do in various contexts. How and when and whom you tell, "I love you" matters a great deal to the meaning; how we say, "That's great!" changes from time and place. Do we say it enthusiastically, ironically, sarcastically, for instance? Or maybe we're just Tony the Tiger.

No, probably not.

So. We speak. We act. In a context that contributes to meaning, we do, always, make assertions, defend them, offer counter-arguments, and try out ideas. We try to find possible meanings, and which is best — nearest to reality. We do the same things with the next word, the next, the next.

We know this as thinking, reading, speaking. It's how we talk to others and how they talk to us, whether through a book or over coffee, in a class or at the dinner table. If we don't distinguish, in what and where it's said and by whom, nothing makes sense. Sometimes it doesn't anyway — but it's guaranteed not to if we don't do anything.

Scripture, relationship with God, talking to others, and even one word: follow this to the bitter end and we can't know God created the universe, and us in it, in His image. We can't think of it as having been or not been. There is no sure data on Christ. There are no ideas. We'd have no idea.

Absent logic, how can we claim the words on this page communicate — and how can we hope others will understand?

It wouldn't stop there. No history, no philosophy, no science, no math … no nothing. More precisely: *only* nothing.

So we can't even begin to read, not the Bible or a breakfast cereal box, without fixed laws of logic. We also can't talk. We're barred completely from communicating with others, me or God or your dog, in any form.

Now in the moment we may never think of this, and rightly so. We do not necessarily think of the logic of "I love you" — we'd even suggest it's not the best way to proceed in that arena. But it still depends on it even if we never think, no pun intended, about it.

If we move away from logic we lose all information about God, and if we lose that, we lose Him, because we wouldn't be able to know Him to the extent He has shown himself.

If we dump logic, we have a problem, and not just in Houston.

This matters deeply.

Non-rational opposing viewpoints

No wonder, logic is divisive. It touches nerves, and then bounces up and down on them. Relationships aren't easy, and no less so for relationships among words.

So one perspective says, look, there's human logic and human thought, and by definition it's not God logic and God thoughts. "Your ways aren't my ways." At the extreme of this, logic doesn't violate anything: we can't even do it.

Well we certainly affirm we're not God — a good logical, propositional sentence, if we say so ourselves. But we'd add that God would say it too, about us (we're not God) and He'd be saying the same thing we just said.

So sometimes we can say something, and it is a thought God could be, and even is, thinking. Others include "1+1=2" and "These words are not in French" and "God exists" and "Unsullied, snow is usually white."

God is *wholly other* — we affirm that, too. But this means he transcends us — or rather, we descend, relative to him, and rise, only by him. It does not mean he negates or contradicts all we do. God must be in some sense knowable, even if in the teeny tiniest little sense — the widow's mite, we might say — or he can't tell us about himself, including through Christ.

‡

A second non-rational approach is to say God cannot be expressed but only experienced; we don't see truth apprehending logical relationships. To greater and lesser degrees, this is the basis of many religions, such as Buddhism or Shinto, and even one of the "Big Three" Abrahamic faiths: Islam. In Islam, Allah cannot be known and shouldn't even be discussed. You can submit, but you can't know.

Of course God must be experienced. He cannot *only* be discussed and, as C.S. Lewis once put it, He certainly has more to do than just *exist*, let alone do so for our idle entertainment in debate. And surely our way of knowing is completely different from God's, and there are a jillion ways we can't even grasp how he does what he is even now, this very second, doing.

But we can *get it* a little. We can grasp some of the content. We can *see darkly* as Saint Paul said. If we can't, we know nothing, nothing at all. In the end, we will say, with Aquinas as he said of his monumental work, "It reminds me of straw." That will happen, and should, every dang day. "He must increase, and I must decrease."

Yet God *wants us* to know Him, as He has *said*, in Scripture, in nature, and "In the beginning," when was the Word. And if He wants it, then it simply must be the case that *we can* know Him. And if He wants it, then we should do it.

Without this, God becomes mere analogy or less — a mood or a glow with no substance at all. Plus which, we wouldn't even know the thing He was, because we wouldn't know Him at all.

We sense the comfort in saying we can't fully know God. We have *felt* it. We affirm it. We also want to experience God's presence among us — we want to remember our life with God is beautiful grace: his actions in our lives to do all the things we can't do, and they are legion.

We also sense he is intuitive, not solely propositional, and we see him deal with us in this way. Even intuitions must participate in logic: if the intuition suggests something, we begin to ask if it's right, if it matches a real thing. Moreover — *we ask God*. Of what we imagine, we ask, is it so?

We further don't want to worship words, still less so images, of what we think about God. Don't make a god of our ideas about him: idolatry. So we seek our how the ideas in the Bible are God speaking to us — God choosing to unfold himself to us, and often in propositional logic.

Taking all this into account, Christian faith stands above ones that only permit logic, beyond the non-faiths that deny it, and alone in saying God wants us to know him, which we know because of things he's said, done, and, in the Incarnation, become. We say these things make sense, and are part of the logical approach to faith. Seeing God, hearing God, and in the end, knowing God, requires meaning that flows in part from logic.

A certain man had two sons ...

There's a well known propositional statement.

A specific guy had two kids, both male. One did this. The other didn't. The one who did, also did this and this and this but it didn't work. So he decided to come back. His father knew his son would come home, so he waited for him − maybe every day. Met him on the road. Had a party. The second son got ticked off and said some things. The father affirmed parts of it, corrected the other parts, and promised him everything, too.

That paragraph brims with propositions. As a narrative − the parable of the prodigal son − it depends on statements that assert.

But was there even ever a man? Two sons? Reunion?

How many propositions does it take to describe reality?

Depends on the reality, and how you want to describe it.

When Jesus told the tale, He meant to *say something true* about God, the Kingdom, and how to live with the One in the other. Christ wanted us to learn something. For this purpose it doesn't matter if it's made up. In fact it's better if it is fiction − factually uncertain but possibly true − because it highlights what we're saying even more: if words, *even one in a made up story*, don't connect to something deeper, what's the point? Even if Jesus "merely" wanted to tell a good story, *he couldn't have done even **that** if the words themselves don't make sense* from the beginning − *in* the beginning.

What is a son or a sin, a pig or party? What do those words mean?

Going deeper, we ask about the moral of the story.

More than that, *we know to ask* from the start.

Because even the nuttiest philosophers don't − thank heaven − live in the world they claim exists. They all act as if words mean something, and eating food is a good idea, and running full bore off a cliff is not.

‡

There's something happening here, and it brings us full circle to the start of this chapter, our first question, and the beginning: the, "In the beginning ... " of John's Gospel.

One way to read the verse is, "In the beginning was *the logic*, and *the logic* was with God, and *the logic was* God." Now this is 300-350 years after Aristotle, Plato, and Socrates, and they used the term to represent similar things at the time. The term has "baggage" as we say, and John knew it. In the beginning: the logic, the reason, and the law ... of God.

Also consider: it's a Greek word, *logos*, in a Hebrew form. John writes to Greek-speaking Hebrew Christians. He's working in two approaches, encompassing both ... and transcending both.

There is definitely something going on here.

Now try it, as some have, as a hymn. Think of the beginning of John as a good classical hymn, making tightly compacted theological statements. A hymn does that in every verse, even every line or clause.

Also a hymn is moving and stirring and incredible to the heart. In fact, it is this in part *because of* the words. The words are that in part *because of* the propositional logic. It must include logical truth.

When we stand in church and sing to God we're singing propositional praises to Him, telling him things we say are true about Him. We say we love Him, and that's as propositional as "Will you marry me?" It doesn't say it *all* — and there's a lot of feeling and emotion wrapped up in "Will you marry me?" as well.

Hymns move hearts by other than logic. "Music hath charms to soothe the savage breast," we say — and not by a snazzy syllogism it may form. Music touches us, and while we don't mean that concretely we certainly do say it in some sense ... literally.

So again, we may never think of the logic underlying our efforts. We'd best not try to all the questions of life with logic alone. We don't have to. It may be that we sing. Perhaps the lover asking for the woman's hand is going to do the same thing in line with his request. We don't have to say, every time *logic is here.*

What we must do is know that it does underlie the questions, answers, and even the songs. We pay it due respect, neither violating nor denying, and perhaps we even learn how to work with and in it a little.

A man can ask his lady to marry him any way he likes — or rather, any way *she* likes. But first he has to mean it.

Chapter Five: Cornerstones

The professor said he wanted objectivity but this wasn't true. Claiming to leave pesky religious beliefs at home he'd merely substituted hard-hearted and angry skepticism. Moses didn't write the Torah, all prophecies were fudged to fit, and Israel was polytheistic, but crafty monotheists won out. The point wasn't if the views were true: the point is students were simply expected to submit.

One student finally protested: "You're not objective! You're just skeptical!" He left after peers heckled and jeered. A second student stayed until semester's end, and asked what he'd wanted to know from the first week of class.

"Is there a God?"

The professor's answer stunned him.

"I don't know!" He snapped. "I have no idea."

Introduction

Seems a reasonable question in a religion class. He could have said, "No, there isn't, and that relates to some of what've been learning here."

But to have *no idea*?

How can we study scripture (Moses, the prophets, monotheism, say) if we don't ask after God? He's prominent in its pages. Not that it becomes a class on becoming a Christian, but exploring the existence (or not) of a major character *in* the Old Testament could arguably be part of a class *on* the Old Testament.

Now don't worry: this isn't another chapter on scripture. We did that a few chapters back.

Instead, this being a kind of *class* on apologetics we offer (call us crazy) here some key questions on ... apologetics. We want to speak to what the practice involves, and what it can't; what questions it answers, and those beyond its scope. Can't hit everything, but here are a few ideas to start.

Faith is not blind

Faith is first. Apologetics[9] flows from faith.

We want others to know what we believe and this leads to apologetics. It can take many forms — historical and cultural are just two — and such efforts can even strengthen our own faith, as we learn, by the Holy Spirit, more and more of God and His Christ. Apologetics flows from faith, and it in turn strengthens faith.

So faith is strong. That's first. It is a hardy, chesty, muscular, powerful thing. Not a "blind leap" or "God of the gaps" but something that comes after and is based on a ton of hard work. "Faith comes from hearing and hearing from the word of God" — this is not a la-di-da or tra-la-la faith.

Consequently, dump any ideas of faith as *what we believe when we don't have any reasons*. The Christian life, including apologetics, flows from this faith in God — and that isn't weak. We serve the biggest, coolest, onliest God in all the galaxies, and we do so with a faith worthy of that call.

After Christ as God and Man, the reliability of scripture, the centrality of the Resurrection, and the value of logic, we ask what apologetics does and is, and how.

It flows from and strengthens faith.

‡

---

[9] We've been so busy talking about Jesus and Scripture and the Resurrection, we finally get a chance to note that *apologetics* simply means "a defense" or "presentation" — not, as it has sounded to some, an apology. See 1 Peter 3:15, where we're told to be ready to give *reasons*.

Now, faith is trust and confidence, and we put it in what's reliable. It's a car that runs or a dog that barks. It's a pastor who shepherds — we put our trust in people and places proven reliable. We sit on chairs that don't break and grandmothers who can bake. Faith has its reasons, too.

Point being: evidence is in favor of faith, not against it. We trust what's trustworthy. The faith-reason divide is arbitrary and false, and a part of a strong apologetics is connection to real, vibrant faith.

The Christian faith, apologists assert, is reliable. The evidence in favor, seen and unseen, ends up being more than enough. Clearly there's work to do, yes it must be shown as best we can, surely we examine questions and entertain objections and consider issues — all of this. We don't see it all now, and we don't have to (we rarely have 100 percent certainty in all we do) but yes, faith … apologetics … faith … a full and virtuous circle.

So we don't mind being asked for proof. In fact we want to be asked.

We *want* to seek that evidence. Remember: it strengthens our faith.

Take this book, for instance. It's just a start, sure, but we think it can be a good one. We're hoping — and working — to show evidence for many important things readers and others need to think about. Much of it will also lead, we pray, to stronger belief, that is, to action. None of this, you may notice, has to do with hiding evidence, or shunting aside an honest, heartfelt question, or even any objections.

Evidence matters to apologetics, and evidence matters, period.

Scripture calls us to believe on evidence, for instance. It says that's how to approach scripture *itself*. Recall an earlier comment, where we learned scripture questions itself; not only that, but it tells us to do so, too.

Christ cared about evidence, too. He didn't think faith was excluded in reason. It certainly transcends it, but it does not *ignore* it, still less counter it. If Jesus didn't care about evidence, why did he give so much of it? The man could've done us a favor — at least made the Bible shorter — by just showing up after the Resurrection (with no proof of *that* of course) with a *Hey guys, just believe in me, K? You guys good with that?*

Come to think of it, this book would be a lot shorter, too.

If all faith is blind, why not just believe anything? Go be a Christian, a Muslim, an atheist, or Napoleon. Doesn't matter. But in truth, all people believe *something* and anyone who says "let's not consider these beliefs," is first, not living true to their supposed reason and rationality (rational seekers of truth don't arbitrarily shut off entire avenues of enquiry). The second thing he's doing is considering *another* set of beliefs instead, and possibly not even acknowledging this. Discounting religious beliefs isn't "rationally neutral" (as the professor in our true example claimed) but is rather a position on the validity of holding religious belief — which as it happens, can be held for very good reasons indeed.

Big pictures

It comes down to how we see the world — meaning how we answer the "big picture" questions. Faith comes first. Then come the questions.

Take a well-known example from a man we're mentioning often, with good reason: Professor C.S. Lewis. He asked three well-known questions about ships to illustrate our most important issues.

Each *ship* in his example is a person, and Lewis said each ship must be seaworthy, it must not hit other ships, and it must know why it's sailing.

These are all questions related to ethics of one sort or another, including an overall view of how to live. Others ask other questions that all people answer in one form or another: Who am I? Why am I here? Who is good and how do I become a good person? What is my problem? What is the solution? How much time do I have? And so on.

Like noses and sin natures, everyone has these questions.

Apologetics also depends on such ideas, which we've prepared as five questions. Like faith, these "cornerstone" answers help us *do* apologetics — and like faith they help us live.

- *Origins* — where did we come from?
- *Meaning* — why are we here?
- *Identity* — who are we?
- *Morality* — how should we live?
- *Destiny* — where are we going?

These questions develop an apologetic and a life. Like contact lenses or eyeglasses — or laser surgery if it goes deep enough — they help us see.

Origins are huge. If there's no God and we're a product of chance, our origins are beyond humble, on their way to irrelevant. But Christians say God intended us, created us with meaning, and thus has ideas on how to live, and to begin with, how we should live with Him.

Meaning is the purpose question[10]. Why are we here? What had God in mind when he created us — it came before his actual creating. That's big. God planned us and set us in motion. He had reasons, He wanted us, and He made it happen. He gave us His image[11], and we lived. We have

---

[10] An older, and Greek, word for *purpose* is *telos* ... *The Telos-Driven Life*, anyone?
[11] An older, and Latin, word for *image of God* is *imago Dei* ... *Imago Dei Driven Life*, anyone?

work to do that no one else can — individually and collectively. Remember the sailing ships. There's purpose in having the image of God.

Clearly this has much to do with *Identity*. We're made in his likeness so we're worth something. We must live accordingly, and treat others in the right ways because *they* are created in God's image as well. Thusly made, we begin to ask, what defines us *as* humans? What is essential; what can we learn as we toddle along? Can we learn which is which? How much of identity is fixed, and how much malleable[12]?

Morality is that issue of not bumping into the other ships. How should we live? If God exists and in certain ways, He has some claim on us, and our answers to the five questions. In morality God is the core: He sets the standards. He grounds it, gives it, and shows us the way we can become humans who naturally keep those standards He sets.

Finally, *Destiny* — our end — is vital, because if the universe will just … end … in a fiery cataclysm or the final cold eclipse of the last star in a billion galaxies — well it doesn't matter much, right? From first oblivion to last, the blind lead the blind until we fall into the cosmic ditch. But a Christian apologetic says no, there is no end, and we will worship God, in Trinity and unity, forever.

Apologetics offers answers to those questions, and as such contributes to an overarching story, sometimes called a worldview, sometimes called Christianity. It's not just a worldview, of course, but it is that.

---

[12] No Greek or Latin here. Just a note to say Christians ask about *meaning* before *identity*, as we believe *purpose* precedes *who we are*. One element of a worldview called existentialism is the reverse: identity comes first, and we create our own meaning. These are different ideas.

All this matters. If our *origins* are from God, and he gives *meaning*, via His image, then our *identity* is to some degree fixed, and we must behave *morally*. This leads to our *destiny*, to how things end ... if, in fact, they do.

Good answer! Good answer!

But whether it ends or not, Christianity does answer the questions now, and apologetics offers reasons those answers are good. There are other worldviews, too, since there are other answers to the five questions.

We mentioned *existentialism*, and that's one way of looking at it. We originated, period, and we're here now, human, and we have to make our meaning. It's identity first, and if we don't do it, life is going to be nasty, brutish, and short — at least we hope. So maybe we can make a kind of meaning by how we live. Sorry, no objective purpose, but let's try and define one. We'll each define it differently, but forget about the grand scheme of things, because there isn't one. No destiny, either.

Could try *scientism*; many people do. Religion isn't a good way to go, this says, because the origin was the big bang and the destiny is candle snuffing, or unending growth, depending on whom you ask. Faith isn't going to save you and was never meant to, and it's not just Christianity; no faith is true or false. What is? What's the meaning? Science says. The right way to meaning is pursuit of knowledge, defined as facts. Identity isn't fixed and neither is morality.

These views, and others, tend to be so deeply ingrained, laser surgery is needed for mere correction, let alone seeing well. They make claims to the same kinds of answers as faith offers — in fact, they require faith of their own, since we can't, for instance, scientifically verify philosophical underpinnings of science, or figure out a deeply true way of saying, in an existentialist universe, why we shouldn't just kill everyone, or ourselves.

We're also not discussing all possible answers to our five questions, all possible worldviews, and we're not saying there's zero value in any here or not here. As we noted earlier in this chapter, we're committed to what the evidence shows. As Christians we also honor existentialist desires for an honest, authentic life. It has always been thus in our faith.

We did it *because* of our origins, because we're created in God's image, because of what flows from that, because morality matters, and because we're headed somewhere very specific, and very important.

‡

Ever done a jigsaw puzzle? Puzzles can be hard no matter what — but they're impossible without the box. We have to know what it's supposed to look like. With it we order the pieces, usually starting with the borders — the boundaries — then filling in the details. The picture on the front of the box guides us, and the work takes shape before us, and soon we have a unified whole.

We believe on evidence and work out answers to the big questions — we fit the puzzle pieces together, guided by a worldview — and a fully orbed picture of life develops.

Along the way, we must see if there *is* evidence, and we must answer the big questions, because the most vital question of all is … God? When we see God *is* and begin to see what he's like, answers to other questions, on salvation, morality, what to do while we're here, and so on, get a little clearer. This is not to descend, like Icarus, into hubris; it is simply to live.

God is at the center of the picture on our box.

Chapter Six: Compulsions

We could be wrong.

*William Lane Craig has said evidence for God's existence isn't like mathematical proof; it's not that sort of thing. Not that it's not good evidence but that it's not that **kind** of evidence.*

It's still evidence. Evidence of guilt in a capital murder trial isn't the same as the evidence that water evaporates, but it can still get someone executed. Heck, a civil trial doesn't ask the same jury unanimity as criminal ones. Evidence of rain may have a lower bar to meet than evidence of love.

Christ calls for not only different kinds of evidence but all kinds. We humans are complex, contrary, and complicated, and Christian faith appeals on many levels. What compels one may not compel another.

Introduction

Some of those compulsions are here.

The last chapter dealt with two "cornerstones" of apologetics: faith and questions. This leads to vibrant faith, which then strengthens apologetics — a virtuous circle. Then we briefly checked two other worldviews; then some results of those.

This chapter offers "compulsions" — a few good reasons to say faith, a Christian faith, tops all others. These aren't specific answers to doctrines, or questions — the Trinity, say, or what kind of baptism is best. It's more like some general ways Christianity meets life in all its complexities.

So this chapter is an apologetic (feel free to delve deeply in these areas and use them your own darn selves) as well as giving you some ideas of what apologetics can do.

Like we said: faith flows into apologetics … apologetics leads to faith.

The three concepts we introduce are *reality, knowledge,* and *existence.*

Reality shows

It's real.

We begin again on worldview[13].

Worldview apologetics says *reality is a simple reason for believing in God.* If we can get any kind of handle on the idea of reality — let alone reality itself — then, says this approach, we'll be on our way to belief.

Worldview is simply "how one sees the world at large."[14] If we get to rock bottom, we'll get to something we can't prove, since if we did, um, where did that come from? We're going to get to *axioms,* the bedrock of interpretation that not

> **Basically**
>
> Beliefs come from other beliefs, but some beliefs are foundational and don't depend on other beliefs for justification. These *properly basic* beliefs are outside the realm of belief.

only don't need explaining: they can't be.

In short, there are true things (math theorems, say) we can't guarantee with empirical data, inductive reasoning, or a syllogism. At some point, as Tug McGraw used to say, *Ya gotta believe.* We must trust eyes and guts or at least accept the laws of logic. We can't prove what we use to prove everything else.

As pastors say, the Bible doesn't prove God: it assumes Him.

For instance, the scientific method holds up because somewhere along the line it was first *assumed,* then tested, then it did really, really — *really* — well on what it can do, whereas alchemy … not so much. We can't get

---

[13] For more, see *20 Compelling Evidences That God Exists,* by Ken Boa and Robert Bowman.
[14] *Without a Doubt: Answering the 20 Toughest Faith Questions,* by Ken Samples.

gold from coal. Try all day, and all we'll get is night.

That assumption was its starting point, and if we'd waited for them to prove the assumption, we'd still be waiting.

So some *beliefs* precede our *rational* view that our senses measure truth. This makes the Scientific Method possible, not to mention enabling us to enjoy Fettuccini Alfredo. This puts both in the realm of *reality*. Neither do we sense the mind, nor can we prove neurons fire without firing them. It involves assumptions, and they're darn good ones. Properly basic beliefs correspond to reality with no help from us and we're cool with that. The next time one doesn't correspond thusly, head for the nearest exit.

Know what I mean?

We can know.

We can know, and we can know that we know. We can know, and we can know that we know, and we can know that we knew, and we can tell others also. We can be right, and wrong, and partly either. Sometimes we aren't sure; sometimes surely clueless. We're rarely 100 percent right, but that's almost never required — whether driving a car, drinking water, or voting for president. We can temporarily apprehend (cramming enough, just, to pass that physics test) or we can truly, deeply, interactively, fully, almost, know and be known (our deepest desire, as it happens). And we can sit at the feet of One who knows, and stand corrected when wrong.

Ain't knowledge grand?

Because if we can know, there must be something matches up with the reality of the universe — the first compulsion — and thence and thus the galaxies beyond number or worlds wherever they may be … maybe they can someday be … known.

Or go the other way. If there is reality and reality is, well … *really* real, then the table is a table and that chair is a chair. I have a cell phone, and this laptop, and you have this book. Gel pens and Sharpie markers — in fact they are really cool. And dogs love us and drool, and cats ignore us and scratch, and our husbands and wives are each the most exquisite of all the creatures God hath made, not to mention our children.

So we must have something that allows us to see tables and chairs and pens and books and husbands and wives … rightly. There is information and there is intelligence, and perhaps even love, and once we can get to *those*, then there is maybe, possibly, just perhaps … God.

Haven't proven it by any means, but that's the neighborhood we're in.

That neighborhood is going to borders. Parameters and boundaries — but no, we haven't shown *what* they are just by showing *that* they are. It comes later. We're on big picture compulsions here. A red rose compels, and quite well once we can really see it; for now, we must be content on reality and knowledge.

So here's a table made of wood. Here's a Honda Accord and it's blue, a shiny metallic blue. Run your hand over the surface — but don't buy it, if they try to rip you off.

Can't get any deeper than *blue*, whether in the ocean or the eyes. Don't try to describe blueness; go sell crazy somewhere else. That car is blue. It is very, very, very blue. Its blueness is beyond dispute.

In short: there is a reality and we can know it.

Christianity provides grounds for knowing the reality that's out there, the only *out there*, there is. It says we can apprehend it, and live into it. In many cases, other worldviews don't say this. Some say reality is illusory; others that it's real but we can't know it at all (which means our thought of it is mere fancy at best). On neither approach could any worldview be sure *their* idea was correct, but they'd embrace that concept too, denying and denying and denying reality and knowledge until they don't have a significant amount of anything to work with.

‡

So what are people saying when they're saying such things. It's OK to believe it is rot, since it is, but you can't exactly tell them that, usually. In most cases, you'll need an answer.

"That's just your belief. This one's mine and that one's yours and never the twain shall meet."

Tag. You're out[15].

In truth, to say, "That's your truth," is a way of saying, "I don't know. I'm not sure what to say now, but I know what I'm supposed to say and by the way, buddy, get bent."

That's OK. We've been told not to talk religion at parties: an idea with some merit. But know this, no pun intended: we have the same beliefs — we just frame them differently. We agree about blue (or red or white); we even agree about sitting on chairs and falling in love. We might not agree on all the interpretive bits — is blue a color we find most lovely? Is that a good dog? The difference is perspective, and it's big; but knowledge still … is.

---

[15] Fortunately for all concerned, no one actually lives like this. People believe in chairs and dogs and love, and they proceed accordingly. But sometimes they'll sound like they don't.

But sir, the universe exists

We exist.

This is the shortest bit in the chapter. It's hard to deny we exist.

Older thinkers marveled, "Why is there something and not nothing?" And they knew, as sometimes we affect not to, that they could only ask and answer the question by being there in the first place.

There is something. There is something and how do we explain it?

One of those older thinkers, Richard Swinburne, remarked how it's strange indeed that anything exists at all. But if anything does, it's far more likely to be God in his magnificent simplicity, than the universe with all its complexity, and no God to explain it.

Had to come from somewhere. Maybe we are wrong on whence it did come — but give us something better. Otherwise, the universe exists.

In fact, because it's so simple and indisputable, we get weird objections to it. People talk of primordial soup struck by lightning, or aliens landing and doing pretty much what Jesus did, only it wasn't Jesus. The multiple universes spontaneously existing and dying, an infinite number popping in and out of existence, eventually you get one like ours, you see?

Right. Or God.

Jesus, again

We lied. There are four parts. But in fairness, Christ is not a concept.

Once again, the best reason for faith is … Jesus.

Most explosive character in history, closest and deepest relationship to what came before, most powerful effects ever … Jesus.

Here's a guy who split time. He showed up, and we started a new way of talking about what year it was. It's on every license plate, as Frederick Buechner has noted, and it's not just for Christians but the world. Even if we say "B.C.E." (Before Christian Era) and "C.E." (Christian Era) instead of B.C. and A.D., it's still ... Jesus.

If it seems like the world is measured by distance from or nearness to the life and teaching of Jesus, it's because it is. He is the warp and woof of life. He has formed the way the world works. In all areas you care to name: personal, political, social, economic ... Jesus.

Also he died for you.

If we're just looking out for our genes, we wouldn't die for anyone. If it isn't real, and we can't know and we don't even exist ... fuhgeddaboutit. We'd just be trying to reproduce and we'd kill anyone that gets in our way — taking their stuff when they're dead. If one of our kids died, shame about that, but we can just make another one looks just like him.

But we don't live that way. We simply don't.

Station Break: Being Nice

We can be unprepared, we can have goofy ideas we call reasons, we can make leaps of non-faith even when it's not all that dark. We can do all those things. And we can be mean.

OK, we admit that sounds goofy. It's shorthand for bad apologetics, where we want to make a point or be the center of attention, we're unloving and ... mean.

Now we can be evidentialists or presuppositionalists or Red Sox fans (see the next chapter for two of those). We can do apologetics, historical or cultural. We can sing old hymns or worship choruses. But for goodness' sakes ... play nice.

We tell people they need to know the one true God and Jesus Christ whom He sent. We show them the Kingdom is at hand and they're welcome to come in ... that they may even take it forcefully, if need be.

There is a God, we're responsible to Him, and here's how.

Then we behave beastly and blow the whole deal.

The key word is **winsome.** *We discuss* **that** *in chapter seven too.*

We put rocks in their shoes, as Greg Koukl has said of apologetic arguments — blisters for the gospel, so to speak — but we **do not throw rocks** *at them. We hate the sin, not the sinner; we tangle with the argument, not the arguer.*

We can think ideas dopey, but never that we're talking to a dope. We can't get hacked off at the sheep, not even the annoying one who went and got hisself lost.

This is seed sowing — or rock-strewing, if you prefer. We sow a seed and do some good. We move on to the next furrow. Maybe we come back and check on the young shoots, put down some water (occasionally fertilizer, no doubt). It's hard work as any farmer can say.

But we never forget we're playing on God's team, and we play nice. We don't worry: if we move the ball down the court, we can expect him to score. Just feed Him the ball and watch. There is **no pressure.**

It frees us up to be nice.

Chapter Seven: We Apologize

C.S. Lewis says the irresistible and the indisputable are the two weapons God's nature forbids him to use. It means essentially that he won't force us to believe: "He cannot ravish; he can only woo."

We concur: God is a gentleman. He will draw us as close as we'll allow. If we want to follow Him we may. Whosoever will may come. If we want to live after God, in love, and be close, have that intimacy ... He wants it, too, and first.

If not, He will comply. He will not in the end go where He is not wanted.

But what, exactly, do we do, to help draw more to Him?

More than one pastor has noticed how much time he spends trying to "get" us to church ... while in the New Testament, Jesus is running away from them!! In Mark's very first chapter the men tell Jesus, "It is going great! **Everyone** *wants to see you!" and Jesus says ... "Let's leave." Elsewhere He's escaping in boats or hiding in the desolate places or commanding people not to talk about Him.*

Not exactly, **Always be ready to give a defense.**

On the other hand, "Go into the world and make disciples" has worked OK as church growth. So yet again, Jesus is a reasonably intelligent guy, and we're ... wondering what that means for us.

He knew what He was doing. But what do we say, now?

That's the question of this chapter: what should we as apologists say? How do we carry out the apologetic enterprise? What do we do?

Introduction

So with ... apologies ... to St. Francis, "Preach the gospel at all times, and sometimes we're prolly gonna need words."

But, we ask, which ones?

And if we know anything about apologists, we're going to follow that question with ... *why?*

Go

First, we must.

Before we get to why and what and how, be clear at least on this: God says enough about being able to show and tell our faith that it's clear we are supposed to do it.

Consider:

• *"Beloved, although I was eager to write to you about our common salvation I found it necessary to write asking you to contend for the faith."* — Jude 3. Jude says he swapped his first goal for a new one because the ungodly were perverting God's grace and denying Christ.

• *"Walk in wisdom toward outsiders, making the best use of the time. Let your speech always be gracious, seasoned with salt."* — Colossians 4:5-6. Paul says do this to know *how to answer* each person. Just before this he asks for an open door to preach the mystery of Christ, with clarity.

• *"Honor Christ the Lord as holy, always being prepared to make a defense to anyone who asks for a reason for the hope that is in you."* — 1 Peter 3:15. The full passage goes farther.

Jude, Paul, and Peter agree: contending for the faith is vital, surpassing even the chains of prison on the list of present concerns, and based in our love and service for the Lord.

Each passage also incorporates imperative tones, and sometimes this is direct. So they aren't recommending a hobby, but commanding a duty. A primary motivation is God decrees it. What else is good about it? Loving.

We forget that second one sometimes, but look at the passages again.

Jude is intense, and he speaks to the *beloved*. That is you and me and all who enter the Kingdom, which is the whole point: helping them come in.

Paul says to be wise, gracious, and clear, and he's in chains! Peter is no easier on our doltish, oafish, churlish behavior: be willing to suffer (Paul) and sanctify Christ (Peter) and speak with gentleness and respect.

If we don't do it with love, nothing matters.

Go we must ... in love.

Preach

Words, words, words ... stick with words.

An earlier note ... noted ... that the word *defense* in 1 Peter is, in Greek, *apologia* — meaning, "to defend, speak, or

> ## Counsel For The Defense
>
> *It's not simply "Always be ready" nor is it just, "to give a defense." It's not even mainly about "the hope that is within" us. It's this —*
>
> "Who is there to harm you if you are zealous for what is good? But even if you should suffer for righteousness' sake, you'll be blessed. Have no fear of them, nor be troubled — but in your hearts honor Christ the Lord as holy, always being prepared to make a defense to anyone who asks you for a reason for the hope that is in you; do it with gentleness and respect, having a good conscience, so when you are slandered, those who revile your good behavior in Christ may be put to shame. Better to suffer for doing good, if it's God's will, than for doing evil." — 1 Peter 3:13-17

reply." It's what we do here at Apologetics.com: *give a defense for the true claims of Christianity*. Sounds as if we're sorry, like an apology, right? Sorry ... no. It's another word for *reason*, as in how a lawyer gives reasons to decide a case this way or the other. There's even a book called *The Apology* (on the trial and death of Socrates) but *that's* not apologizing for anything. It's giving reasons why he believed, and why he chose death before dishonor.

What kind of defense do we offer? We've seen a good defense is not *offensive*. We apologists are not to be cantankerous curmudgeons; we're supposed to play nice with others, and thereby defend *and confirm* the gospel (Philippians 1).

But do we use philosophy? History? Culture? Just scripture? Miracles? Deliverances or discoveries? Science? Do we err in *trying* to "defend" at all — does God need defending?

Yes. Yes. Yes. Sometimes. Yes. Yes. Yes. No — No.

We need a system.

Fortunately, others have thought of this.

Fortunately there are four, for finding a form.

‡

The following four approaches cover most of the ground. If we do any apologetics, we're probably doing one or more of the four, whether we'd realize it or not. Here they are:

1. Classical/Evidential

2. Presuppositional

3. Cumulative Case

4. Reformed Epistemology

Let's put some flesh to each of this: pros, cons, and other neat stuff. It's OK if you don't get everything: we're just introducing some ideas here. It is some ways to talk about God to people who need to know him.

We may be mostly familiar with the *classical/evidential* approach: giving scriptural basis for belief plus general evidence. Apologists working here include people like Norman Geisler, J.P. Moreland, William Lane Craig, Doug Geivett, Richard Swinburne, and R.C. Sproul, among others.

Here you get cosmological arguments, the reliability of Resurrection, a historicity of the Gospels, and Jesus' divinity. Some of the chapters in the book you're reading would come under this heading. Also included here are philosophical approaches (such as Thomas Aquinas and his work) or teleological thought, such as intelligent design.

There's a significant reliance on external confirmation, which contrasts with the presuppositional approach, below. This external confirmation is a strength of classical/evidential apologetics, because credibility can be a given: people may connect with philosophy, science, or history, since the disciplines are recognized as valid. So if Christianity is reliable there, it is believable. There's also good scholarship by Christians and real evidence to be offered. It carries weight.

This is also a weakness. If man is sinful, this will affect thought and life — including a life of scholarship. We're unsaved to start with, and it will, inevitably, affect our work. Christians working in this area might do OK. But what about the hearers — will they be able to receive it? And can we start with externality and get to God at all? Won't we miss the mark?

Here's another question: given its limitations, and if we can't get to the One true God, what do we get? Will it just be theism? If we prove design, will we simply end up with a designer, perhaps of watches?

Classical evidentialists would say it's OK because it's a first step and a good start. They'll agree we can't argue people into the Kingdom but we can clear some brambles. It doesn't prove *Yahweh* and atheists can laugh, point, and die in unbelief. Except that it's theism, and the atheist will not be laughing by then.

It doesn't prove the whole shebang, but maybe it proves enough, or it disproves something else, or it generally shifts someone a little closer to the door of the Kingdom of God — Jesus Christ.

‡

Presuppositionalism reverses this, while not excluding it. It begins in a different place, but overlaps. If classical evidentialism brings us nearer the door, presuppositionalism starts inside the room.

This one says behind everything we're trying to prove, everything we believe, are beliefs we already hold: presuppositions. We believe not just before we try to tell or explain anything, but even before we try to know things ourselves. For apologetics, we must examine our presuppositions and, crucially, try to get "inside" of others' prior assumptions.

A Christian taking this tack starts with scripture: the Bible speaks truth about humanity *first*. A corollary to this is: people who don't presuppose can't get very far in a discussion. It may be literally impossible because it is a completely different way of knowing.

If you've ever talked with a non-Christian and felt as though you were talking past each other … maybe you were.

A strength: it stands for the truth of scripture from the outset — even to the point of saying we can't talk at all if we don't agree on this. Faith in Christ is self-consistent and as such has tremendous power to explain, and to give meaning to everything. This not only acknowledges this, but trumpets it. It counters the sometime failure of classical evidentialism to allow for our sin affecting reason, let alone our desire to know truth.

It doesn't rule out using reasons, lofic, or other such efforts; it says you can't start there. It sees such tactics as helpful supplements, but not a full strategy. Finally, a friendly presuppositionalist (yes, there are some) may try truly to understand the presuppositions of an opponent, and this is a humane thing.

The downside is it falls more easily to soft postmodernism. If all we do or say starts from worldview, and no one can simply *see* a thing as it is — and presuppositionalism agrees on this — then everyone has a grid, and we're *all* just talking around and over and past each other. Everyone has a set of beliefs. There may be no reason to talk to each other at all. Not all who practice this method go this far, but that is the danger.

On a more practical level, what can we even say? As we wondered for the start of this chapter, what words do we use? Well, if a Christian says, if you don't start from right principles you can't speak at all, and the guy we're talking to says the same thing about us ... end of discussion.

‡

The *cumulative case* apologetic is how many would think of their faith, were they asked. Perhaps we would think of how we were raised and/or our lives before following Christ. We consider reasons we came to Christ in the first place. Now we, "just look around," and see a confirmation of our beliefs in many areas and ways. This is a cumulative case.

It involves evidence — in fact, quite a bit of it, expanding what counts as evidence, and seeing confirmation of Christ in different ways, the arts, for instance. As the evidence gathers, *accumulates*, the case is made. So, a good book or movie or painting revealing the truths of human nature ... plus material in our DNA strongly suggesting design ... plus a historical case that Jesus existed and left his mark on the world ... equals faith.

Toss in astronomy, beauty, common morality, doing the math — and mathematics itself — and you have a good "case for Christ," as it were.

In fact, Lee Strobel's work would probably fall under this approach: the basic idea being look, the probability of this is overwhelmingly in favor of the Christian account of life, the universe, and nearly everything.

It's not a knockdown, drag-out, ironclad formal syllogism — but it's great inductive reasoning. One argument by itself, eh, whattya gonna do? But put 'em all together and *now* what are you going to do? About Jesus Christ, Son of God, Savior? Take all the competing ideas from any and all comers (hey — don't forget miracles!) and Christian theism is on top, ahead, and first.

In short, what's the weight of the evidence?

Problem: cumulative case has to admit at least the chance Christianity is false. If miracles are denied, and design is relegated to blind faith in a blind watchmaker, what's left? In addition, if the "harder" evidence can be tainted by man's sin, what about movies and music? Won't they have even less power? Find a determined non-believer arguing accumulation, and the best we get is a tie. At least we both like books, though.

The biggest advantage is definitely the preponderance of the material. Since so many things *do in fact* point to Christ, talking about the vastness of it can be awesome in power. And people who won't talk to a "presup" fellow or don't want to get into philosophy, may talk books and film and beauty and nature.

This is where most of us actually live: our families, politics, or cultural pursuits, plus the media, economics, and so on. So there's a lot of ground to consider common, and that can be good.

Anyway, it's another approach.

‡

Reformed epistemology is relatively recent. It takes a novel idea and says it strongly from the start: that belief in God is "properly basic" (like basic beliefs in a previous chapter) and can be simply … done. That is, we can believe, *period*. We don't need arguments for belief in God, and it doesn't have to be justified. We can have foundational belief, and there's nothing illogical or counter-factual or unreasonable. Cosmological arguments are swell and transcendental stuff is great but we can actually begin without it.

These are men like Alvin Plantinga, Nicholas Wolterstorf, and William Alson, among others. They're scholars all, with one hardcore apologetic, though perhaps they wouldn't consider it one.

Do we *show* Christianity is true or do we *know* it's true?

We can talk to people on this basis, and we don't have to give ground to a skeptic. There's just as much reason to start from belief, as unbelief. So this is a vibrant, confident faith, sure of what a man or woman in the Kingdom can be sure of, and no less able to share Christ than anyone.

The caveat here is that it can be subjective. If not, it could definitely be thought subjective by people we deal with.

In other words, for the individual Christian, we know. Fine and fair. But maybe it took 30 years to get to that point so how do you "explain" three decades of faith? G.K. Chesterton has said it's harder to say why we believe the things we most deeply hold — precisely because we so deeply hold them.

If someone asks us to say why we're Christians, we might sputter, "But … look at that tree! … And answers to prayer!?! … And … have you met my wife? She's lovely — how could I *not* believe!"

As you can see, it's not something you can teach, or even learn, except personally. And for good or ill, it won't hold much water with the cynic, or even an honest seeker who wants to know why this or that.

Do

Just do it.

Well, OK — don't *just* do it. But do it.

A definite difficulty with all this analysis, is if we get really good at it — talking a good game, say, Monday morning quarterbacking everyone else's game — we never get into the game. Rather, be doers of the word, and do not run aimlessly — James and Paul this time. Coupling this and earlier admonitions from Peter, Jude, and, again, Paul, and it's clear the big guns of early Christianity thought there was much for us to do.

It's fun to talk apologetics — history of, methods for, war stories in — and on and on and on. But too many people never do it. We never go *do* apologetics. That's important, and more useful, than finding the perfect method, which is not, strictly speaking, possible.

If a thing is worth doing — Chesterton again — it's worth doing badly.

Paul says even if people preach Christ from envy, praise the Lord, and pass the popcorn, because this is going to get good. We paraphrase here.

Short version: don't let our talk hinder our walk in this way, either.

Let's go about, not just think — or talk — about it.

Christians: shut up and deal.

Definitely.

Chapter Eight: Moral Miracles

To understate the matter, the Lord we serve is fond of paradox.

The last shall be first, the first last ... wise as serpents, harmless as doves ... to rule is to serve, serving is ruling ... if you want to live you have to die ...

He also said, not quite paradox but something to make sense of, the adulterous demand signs (Matthew 12 and 16, Luke 11) ... then in John 10 He says believe because of the signs.

This book, which now is half-done, is on thinking and doing. There's debate among Christians on which is bigger. Our answer is both ... a paradox. Such family squabbles are good, assuming they're irenic not polemic; assuming we don't lose sight of our responsibility in this life: to hear and obey.

Introduction

We can't argue them into the Kingdom.

This is surely an odd thing to say after half a book of reasons.

Yes we can clear brush or put rocks in shoes; heck, we can do both. But ultimately it's a matter of the heart. Christ said that from the beginning, many times over, and of course it's still true today. It's one thing He said that's not paradox. It's one point, with no reversal: love from the heart.

It's the heart.

To hear and obey are heart issues. Do we have the plowed ground of a teachable heart — "ears for hearing" — and the humility to respond, and to follow when he speaks, when he beckons?

Miracles and morality are heart issues. They each ask, *will we hear* and *will we obey*? It's funny, paradoxical, how these two areas fit together, as the shorthand version of *miracle* for many people is, "that which cannot occur" while the quick-and-dirty definition of *morality* is, "that which all should do."

Can't believe it

The first problem with miracles is we know they can't happen.

The second problem with miracles is that they do.

Miracles violate natural law — *ergo* ... no miracles. But as Galileo said, *eppur, si muove* — "And yet, it does move." So sometimes, there it is. We have testimony, reports, anecdote, personal experience, Gospel accounts.

We have *plausibility structures*, to use the five-dollar phrase.

Plausibility structures are a range of pre-existing beliefs making certain ideas possible. UFOs are going to be more accepted in a certain place and time, and among certain people, than others. Same with miracles: people in certain circles will reject them out of hand because of their beliefs. Yes, this is related to the idea of *properly basic*, discussed earlier in the book — you're doing great!

So is a miracle like a UFO? No, it's merely that some people are more open to one thing, some to another, and some will disbelieve before the evidence is even examined. That is not, as should be clear from this book and what Apologetics.com has tried to be about for more than a decade, a good way to start.

What's a good way to start?

Defining terms of course. What is a miracle, for instance? In a broadest sense a miracle is an *irregularity*. There are regular patterns, but miracles are exceptions — they are, literally, exceptional. Call them anomalies but don't call 'em impossible. Because the definition of an *exception* includes saying it's rare, unlikely, and not the rule. That's why it's an exception.

Storms do calm. Rain goes away for years and returns. There's nothing *contrary* about loaves and fishes becoming more loaves and fishes — it is what pumpernickel and mackerel do. Know what else? There is nothing *essentially contradictory* with God becoming man. Given a God and given man, what's the problem? Now showing God, assuming it can be done, is another question; we're simply saying miracles should not, must not, be dismissed before they're even discussed.

So ... anomaly, irregularity, exception — but that doesn't mean it can't happen. It doesn't even mean it's abnormal.

Miracles can be common events happening in uncommon ways, or on different schedules, as with Jesus calming the storm: but storms do calm.

But we tend to make our knowledge of how things usually occur into the rule of how they must always occur. We turn a *description* into some permanent *proscription*. But *probable* — even highly so — is not *necessary*.

There's nothing illogical about that.

In fact, what it actually is, is logical.

Formal deductive logic works on what is logically necessary, and it's a good thing since we call it *logic*. But inductive thought works on what is likely, i.e., not necessary. It *indicates* something may be likely or about to happen again. It may be really, really, really, really, nearly sure to occur. But it's not required.

So the bar is high, but not insurmountable.

So miracles are possible, and unlikely — just as it should be.

So we can give miracles — say, the Resurrection — a look, a once-over, a series of tests to see if, now that they can happen, whether or not it did. The English call this a *fair cop*. We just call it fair, and we have no issue in asking, and taking, an honest assessment of miracles.

We're *imago Dei* Christians here ... apologists or budding ones, and we want this. They said there was no God. We said well maybe there is, and here's why. Maybe no Resurrection, maybe logic isn't a big deal, maybe I can't see any foundations ... they said. So we should a bit about that.

So now it's miracles. They don't violate rules; they're rare exceptions to them. First someone will say miracles are impossible. We show how they aren't. We show they logically could occur, we line that up, and lay it out — how they could occur, and how maybe they did.

There's a God and there are miracles; not a huge step to say he does them. He's active in his creation, neither blind nor uncaring. These we can show, as well.

Once we get to a point where someone says, OK, there might be God — man, that's golden. Maybe the naturalism will keep flowing, but the chink is in the armor, the pinprick is in the dike. Yeah, even if we were levitating in front of the guy he's going to put it on some other reason: *Even if a man rises from the dead, some will not believe.*

It's a heart issue.

It's the heart.

But at least we've moved to where miracles are at least possible — it's now intellectually irresponsible to dismiss them *a priori*.

Now begins the real work.

Won't do it

It's called life.

We're nearly to part two of the book, where all the awesome thinking we've been doing becomes, well … doing. Thinking is inevitable; we do it even if we deny it — even in denying it (see chapter four). Doing isn't the same. We don't have to *do* anything.

Now the real work begins, which is living it out.

That's morality. It's as denied as miracles, and it's as demanded, and it is as real. It's about God existing (again!) and how he says about matters, in this case moral. If God exists, he meant it. He meant us. And he meant for us to mean it.

We can only owe something to another person. We have no duty to the lawnmower or a piano. If someone lent us the lawnmower or bought our piano, OK. Since a person is involved. We know this, and from the start. I should do this because you did that, perhaps. Obligation. C.S. Lewis is at it again, on this very subject, in *Mere Christianity*. Told you we're close.

That's our daily moment-by-moment morality — and momentous it is, because God is the First Person to do anything, and he has a claim on our actions preceding and superseding all others. He's the most moral being in all the galaxies, the grounding and basis for right and wrong, for good and evil. He started it, he is it, and all the evil we do in this world comes from not listening to us when he speaks about it.

Christians don't have a "problem of evil" because we know why and we know Who. We understand evil is, where it comes from, and why it might be allowed and necessary. The non-believer must make his sense of it, with no grounding for good: why wouldn't evil exist in a world a

God never made and doesn't exist to care about? There's just harm and suffering and pain and death.

Christians, on the other hand, can talk about it, and can offer not only explanation for it, but solutions. Those who decry it from outside, can't. They can't do anything about it.

We can tell, explain — and we can do something.

Hoaxes and hypocrites

Christians make it hard to believe.

On miracles, you get Reverend Pompadour smacking people around: hand to the forehead, coughing in their face, tripping them when no one (they think) is watching. We made that one up but would it shock us if a self-styled healer dialed in on contemporary greeting practice with a fist-bump or a chest thump? Not really.

We believe God heals. But these guys sure make it tough.

Meanwhile on morality, you get Senior Pastor S.O.B. making time with the organist or the worship leader or the deacon's wife or all of the above if you want to know the truth.

How do we present the gospel in such settings?

Hoaxes and hypocrites hurt. False miracles and false morality: we can work through them, but it'd be nice if we didn't have to so much. Yes, it would be nice if we weren't sinners.

Good things are corruptible and nothing is untouched by the fall.

But, yes: we help them work through it, if it matters deeply. Then we power back up and get moving again.

It helps to remember that not only good is *corruptible* — all things are.

It also helps to remember they are *good things* — God can do miracles. Even in morality.

"It's all good" is truer theology than we know. It doesn't always seem the case but in reality — in how things *are* (see chapter six)— yes. It's *all good*, and all good is from God.

Miracles are set off from daily function like diamonds on black velvet. Velvet is uniform and smooth. Until we get to that diamond — which is brilliant and hard. Maybe to God it's part of the whole picture — velvet and diamonds, soft and hard, background and foreground, black, white … we told you he loves paradox.

Morality is the stuff of life, daily function, as maybe no other thing is. It's each decision, every thought-word-deed, all day long. How shall we then live?

Miracles and morality are like God pointing at the moon: one is rare, the other is how we live every second of our lives. God *points* to both — rarely for one, always for the other. He points.

So we look at who's pointing — we look to God — to see if we should look any further. He's our ultimate reference, the Creator and Sustainer of the universe we must learn about.

We also see what he's pointing at. And that moon is so … beautiful.

Then ... *Live*

Chapter One: Why Call Me Good

*We began this book only where it could begin: Jesus Christ. We begin part two in the same place, saying Christ is the standard for all faith **and practice**. We move from "He created all things in heaven and earth" to "In him we live and move and have our being."*

All begins with the God-Man who is the center of all history. Before it begins … God. Before we think our thoughts or do our deeds … God.

*So the main issue in Christian belief is: **God**. If God exists, and we humbly do say he does, based on many good reasons shown in part one, he's clearly going to be the start point here as well.*

So we began our book about thinking and believing with God. We started part one, on thinking, with God. Now we begin part two, on believing, with God.

Whether thinking or believing … begin with God.

Introduction

To *believe* means **to be ready to act as if something were so**.

If we believe our car will start when we turn the key, or the ladder will help us climb higher and hold us steady as we do, or the Boston Red Sox rule, or our spouses are beautiful, we will act in ways to show this: drive the car to work, clean out the rain gutters, hate the Yankees, brag on our spouse.

We believe. We act.

So Christian belief, following on Christian thought, means to be ready to act as if what God says is so. Life and faith include both … apologetics includes both.

What does God say about Christian ethics, about what we do each day to live out — believe — what we think? We're glad you asked.

The Lord is One

Know this: there is one God.

In Mark 12, Jesus quotes from the Shema (Deuteronomy 6) to begin the greatest commandments to, "love the Lord your God with all your heart and with all your soul and with all your mind and with all your strength … and love your neighbor as yourself." The word *shema* means, "Hear" (as in "Hear ye!") and what follows are essential proclamation of Jewish monotheism: "Hear O Israel! The Lord our God, the Lord is one."

Reciting the *shema Yisrael* twice daily is a *mitzvah* or religious duty, and they're often the last words the faithful speak before bed. Parents teach it to children and this truth is part of internal thought and external action.

Christians later put it this way, in The Westminster Confession: *There is one living and true God … infinite in being and perfection.*[16]

One God, perfect, infinitely.

Someone qualified to tell us what for, and how to do it.

Though people tend to trot it out as a new discovery, one of the earliest heresies ever, courtesy of a man named Marcion, said God was not one.

---

[16] The full idea is incredible, inspiring, and quoted here: "There is but one living and true God, who is infinite in being and perfection, a most pure spirit, invisible, without body parts or passions, immutable, immense, eternal, incomprehensible, almighty, most wise, most holy, most free, most absolute, working all things according to the council of His own immutable and most righteous will, for His own glory, most loving, gracious, merciful, long-suffering, abundant in goodness and truth, forgiving iniquity, transgression and sin, the rewarder of them that diligently seek Him, and withal most just and terrible in His judgments, hating all sin, and who will by no means clear the guilty."

It claimed the God of the Old and New Testaments were different. Much can be said about this, and most can't be said here. But some can.

The orthodox Christian belief, what we should be ready to act on, is there's one God. Marcion was the son of a bishop, living roughly from the last part of the first century to the mid-second. He said, simply, the God of the Old Testament was evil, rotten, mean, and nasty, while the God of the New Testament was nice and sweet and good and kind. He also didn't like most parts of either: his canon had about a dozen books.

It's an early duel between "snakes and snails and puppy dog tails" on the one hand, and, "sugar and spice and everything nice" on the other.

To the good, Marcion helped spur the development of the real Canon, as well as to some degree launching systematic theology, since it became important to say for the record what Christians believed.

If this seems arcane and esoteric, it's not: it's crucial. If we say Jesus is God manifest, and we don't know whether God is one, it will be hard to understand Christ's teaching, and even harder to follow it — let alone a perennial problem of whether we should either at all. We need to have a consistency and continuity.

Suffice to say for now that much work exists on God revealing himself at different times, and in different ways, from different angles, and with different emphases. Hence the Old and New, and the untenability of the man named Marcion.

So God is one.

Thinking Christians start with God. Believing ones do, too.

God is one and Christ came. He was God Incarnate, the One True God, and among the reasons he arrived was to reveal fully what God wants. It is about what he wants from us in faith and practice.

Jesus is the visible essence of the invisible God, showing us all we need to see, to do all we need to do. The law and the prophets until John (that Wild Voice, Baptizing Cousin of Christ) were the way in to the Kingdom. Now, says that Christ, it "the violent take it by force."

Now is the time for action.

In the fullness of time

Jesus came not to abolish the law, but to fulfill. This is good news, not least because God's law is a pretty awesome thing that stood in, with, and under the Jewish nation for millennia.

All to the good — but what did Jesus mean by *law*?

Old Testament law can be seen three ways: ceremonial laws, judicial laws, and moral, and this leads to more necessary, essential continuity between Old and New Testaments, in behavior and obedience.

• *Ceremonial laws* are "showings" of Christ crucified, before he came: the priesthood, paschal lambs, temple, festivals and feasts, ceremonial washing and purification, sacrifices, rituals and practices. All showed forth Christ until He came.

• *Judicial laws* were civil regulations in Israel, existing as God's unique creation at that time. Abraham — pagan Chaldean as he was — was plucked from his home, sent on a journey, and turned into a nation, and the nation made laws.

- *Moral laws* are the ones we're most concerned with in ethics: don't lie, cheat, steal, murder, commit adultery, or worship other gods, for instance. Whether eternal, natural, divine, or human, moral law is the one we're still working on today.

Our present, daily responses to these laws differ. We don't practice ceremonial washing or purification; we don't sacrifice animals for our sins. But such laws can still represent the Man who superseded them, and that's one reason we still read the Old Testament: to glean from it, though Christ has come.

> **Do As We Say, And As We Do**
>
> "To be learned and able to discuss the Trinity will get you nowhere if you do not have humility and therefore displease the Trinity." — Thomas á Kempis

The judicial laws were the civic backbone of Israel. It had specific and peculiar properties, civil structure and arrangements that by definition were part of its existence at that time. Christ comes and there's no more place in the New Covenant (or now) for division of lands, the perpetuity of the priesthood, the court system, the monarchy, and so on. Israel came into being to bring forth the Messiah — which it did.

Moral laws may have the strongest claim on us today, yet as we'll see, even these have been superseded in a sense — again by Christ; not that it's now OK to lie or cheat, steal or worship other gods, but that there's something bigger going on here, now that Christ has come.

So Jesus came to fulfill the law.

Why did it need to be fulfilled? What was wrong with it?

The Old Testament law was insufficient, and designed to be. It was meant to be temporary and partial, and it did both those jobs well — leading us as a schoolmaster does, to the cross and to Christ. It's awesome at showing us God's wisdom and righteousness. The law itself is holy, just, and good. At the same, it's not so hot for saving and permanently sanctifying — "no one is saved by the works of the law" is practically a mantra in the New Testament epistles, if Christians were into things like mantras! It sets before us right and wrong, good and evil, but no method for final deliverance from our faithlessness. It was good for what it was good for and useless for what it couldn't do.

It communicates the gospel — but the gospel could not be realized from within the law itself.

That took something — Someone — to supersede the law, to fulfill and culminate it, to make it all make sense, even those weird-sounding parts that even the people trying hard to follow it had trouble with — so much so that they'd devised this Rube Goldberg complex of mazes and false stairways and doorways to nowhere: tripping over the Sabbath and falling into ditches, as a result.

He did this in what He said and did and He did it from the start.

For instance, a primary playing out of the Old Testament moral law, an example of Jesus fulfilling it, is the Sermon on the Mount. Matthew 5-7 is critical for doing Christian ethics by first understanding God's standards for behavior. In fact it's in the Sermon on the Mount where Christ says, "I haven't come to abolish the law and the prophets; I have not come to abolish them but to fulfill." (Matthew 5:17)

Now whatever "fulfill" might mean it won't mean, "do away with." Jesus says it doesn't mean that. Instead it's something like "to fill up" or "bring to fruition" — it's about completion.

But it ain't over. Because He says not one part will pass until all of it has been accomplished, adding that anyone who tries to take part of it away, or teaches others to do so, will be called the least in the Kingdom of Heaven. In fact, our goodness, our righteousness, must exceed that of the scribes and Pharisees. What follows is well-known extrapolation and the extended discussion of hatred and murder, anger and adultery, treatment of others and behavior before God. So we have a law that isn't ended, a command to be perfect, and a heavy-duty delineation of what's expected of us. It doesn't look easy.

But Jesus wasn't making a new law — unless you count the Law of Love. We'll find a fuller discussion of this in our last chapter (on Love, actually) but the "take-away" here is that the One True God has come on the scene in the One Real Man, to bring to full flowering the laws of God that show us how to live.

Why Be Good?

Why be good in the first place?

The final question for now — after, "Is God One?" and "Did Jesus finish the work?" — is why any of this matters, if it does. Keeping the old law was impossible; understanding the new one is difficult … tell us again why we should embark on doing what He wants?

Because God is One and Jesus fulfilled it all.

We respond in obedience to the One True God, Who said so, because of who He is and what Christ did. They've earned it, so to speak (and we can't), and now it's our turn. Westminster again: "Of what use is the moral law to all men? To inform them of the holy nature and will of God, and of their duty binding them to walk accordingly ... "[17]

In short: it matters. What God says about how to live (believe) matters daily. It affects faith, families, finances, fellowships, and freedoms. It matters to how we live and move in church, in the home, at work or purchase, with friends and neighbors, in voting booths ... or whether we vote at all. Shall we do thus and so, go here or there, or something else entire?

Every ethical decision assumes some final authority or standard. The unbeliever considers himself the ultimate authority – even though in practice he's going to submit that to something else, whether it be a formal philosophy, a human leader, an inchoate set of ideas, or etc.

Believers, meanwhile, acknowledge only God holding such authority and prerogative. And again, pay attention to "believer" — since it's specifically about how we shall then live. So the word of the Lord is sole, supreme, and sacrosanct, and it cannot be challenged as the one standard for attitude and action (thinking and believing) in all areas of life. Our obligation to obey can't be judged by any standard that seeks to step beyond or purports to stand above scripture, whether it is history and tradition, or modern feelings and practices.

To link thinking and believing again, it is vital to find the best answers we can — then find the best ways of living those answers out. Pope John Paul II said man's moral autonomy means the acceptance of moral law,

---

[17] The full quotation is thus: "To inform them of the holy nature and will of God, and of their duty binding them to walk accordingly, to convince them of their disability to keep it, and of the sinful pollution of their nature, hearts, and lives, to humble them in the sense of their sin and misery, and thereby to help them have a clearer sight of the need they have for Christ, and the perfection of his obedience." Whew.

of God's command. Human freedom and God's law meet, and are called to intersect: man is meant to freely obey God while God is all about that completely gratuitous benevolence to man.

Now, given our discussion so far — of God and the laws — we might work out at an approach that says, "One immutable God has decreed many laws, which Jesus said He wasn't about to junk, so what we really need to do is obey them, and everything will be Jake."

This would be a bad idea, though perhaps it is sometimes helpful for people to try it

But in fact, Jesus came — as He said — as the *fulfillment* of the law. He is the *culmination* of it. He is, literally, the *crowning* of the law in a Man, who was also God.

Clearly there's something going on here.

Fortunately, Jesus told it what it was.

Go back to the *Shema Yisrael*, the big part *after* "Hear O Israel, the Lord our God, the Lord is One." It goes like this:

"You shall love the Lord your God with all your heart and with all your soul and with all your mind and with all your strength … You shall love your neighbor as yourself. There is no other commandment greater than these."

Love.

Love is the fulfillment of the law.

Something to notice here, to help with the continuity issue (God is One) is that Jesus is quoting Leviticus. The New Testament Messiah is quoting the Old Testament law, connecting the two. God had already told people to love Him and to love their neighbors; they hadn't done so properly — could not do so properly — before Christ.

Love is the fulfillment of the law.

Jesus says as much throughout His final hours with the disciples, telling them early and often and repeatedly to "love one another" and to do so "as I have loved you" and that this will be evidence to all, "if you love one another."

It's love.

So there's something going on here — Jesus is the Jewish Messiah making plain distinctions. He quotes the Old Testament, and has said He came to fulfill the law. He's affirming, interpreting, expanding, all at once. He says the law stands, even as it fades away under His own glory. He's bringing new truth to bear, He's giving new commands, previously unknown yet fully in line with what came before. The Old Testament scriptures are valid, and He endorses them, while giving new shape, character, context, and light.

It's the same, and different.

It's old, and it's new.

Religion and culture are linked in their substance and form, and no culture can hide its religious grounding or its rational formation. Economic and social structures, art and architecture, politics, sports and recreation and leisure — down to the depths of a culture's trauma, longings, hopes, and dreams — are going to be linked to religion.

What we believe.

Which means what we do.

Chapter Two: Admirably Christian

Skeptics often alternate between telling Christians to do what we say we believe with explaining to the rest of the world how impossible it is to do what Christians say we believe. We half-agree with them on this.

*There are ways. We can be good. We can do the right things. It involves, oddly enough, not always **trying** to do the right things. The Pharisee's errors — from trying very, very, very hard to keep the law, do all the right stuff, and tithe our mint, dill and cumin, to helping kill the Christ — are ones we want to avoid.*

In the last chapter, we saw becoming a person who does the right things easily and consistently starts with believing: acting in certain, specific ways.

God is One, we wrote: unified in Himself and thus in His ethics.

Jesus fully showed this, we said: being the way, truth, and life.

We should be good, we concluded. Here's how to start.

Introduction

Remember, "believe" means *to be ready to act as if something were so.*

When we believe we need a little pick-it-up, we'll hit the Starbucks or local indie coffee joint for our caffeine delivery system of choice. A good portion of this book was put together in both types of establishments.

When men and women believe we've found *the one* to marry — we do something about it: asking, or allowing ourselves to be asked.

If God is One, and God is *the* one to be concerned with, and Jesus has spoken (sometimes in word), and if we should now do something about it … what, exactly, do we do?

This.

We believe we must be good and we're ready to act as if it is so.

We believe there's a way to do this and we're ready to do begin.

We believe this way can be taught and learned, and here we go.

Cross, party of one

"Deny yourself, take up your cross, and follow me."

Self-denial is the essence of Christian goodness, the foundation of obedience, the visible manifestation of right behavior. People might not like what we're doing, they might not understand it, but they will know "a prophet has been in their midst" if we deny self. The opposite act — indulging self, worshipping self — is so ingrained, so much the quiet, desperate life of the mass of men, that any alteration or deviation from this norm will — we guarantee it — be noticed.

Self-denial means two things. First, we begin now and today to give it up. Anything blocking our path to God (desires, habits, possessions) … must go. Second, we replace these things with new wants, actions, and items that cement our relationship with Him. With the best in Christian life, there is the negative act, then the positive response: removing what hinders and adding what helps, we start steadily to train ourselves and organize our lives around those things, and only those things, that bring us closer to Christ. These are the first choices of our ethical behavior.

There are tools for this, and it's certainly founded on reading, praying, and worshipping. The "action" of "not-acting" (self-denial) somewhat paradoxically turns out to be pretty extensive — that is, to not do things, requires doing a lot of things. Whatever it takes, it is the sole path to goodness and growth, and we must begin now.

American clergyman Phillips Brooks writes, "The lives of men who have been always growing are strewed along their whole course with the things they have learned to do without," while Scottish pastor George MacDonald (a primary influence on C.S. Lewis) anticipates our maybe-this-is-not-the-right-time cavils, noting, "Alas! This time is never the time for self-denial; it is always the next time. Abstinence is so much more pleasant to contemplate on the other side of indulgence."

> ### Deny Thyself
> The first lesson in Christ's school is self-denial. — Matthew Henry
> Complete abstinence is easier than perfect moderation. — Augustine
> Sacrifice ... is the passion of great souls. — Henri-Frédéric Amiel

English poet Thomas Carlyle says simply, "Great is self-denial!" He adds, in an excellent phrase, "life goes all to ravels and tatters" when we do not practice it. Sir Walter Scott adds that nothing noble or excellent ever existed in one who did not practice "resolute self-denial."

Christian missionary C.T. Studd says simply, "If Jesus Christ be God and died for me, no sacrifice can be too great for me to make for Him."

And this is the key to self-denial: realizing and acknowledging who God is and who we are not. We are "not God" — in the inimitable phrase associated with Alcoholics Anonymous.

Here's another paradox: taking up the cross means knowing we are not God ... so the first step in surrendering our will completely to God and confessing with our hands and feet that we are not God, is when we undergo the very act by which Christ demonstrated He was: crucifixion.

We believe, act, in sacrifice by following after Christ's death.

John Calvin says this ends self-will, projects of personal prosperity, our "avarice and ambition ... frenzied desire ... intrigue for power," which is only restlessness, entanglement, and fatigue. Replacing these equanimity and tolerance, and reliance on God, on whose blessing alone we depend. The wicked depend on their own efforts, gaining no happiness, nothing, and obtaining no blessing. "Surely, men ought not to desire what adds to their misery."

Let go of self to embrace God.

The Consistency of Belief

"The essential thing is a long obedience in the same direction."

This phrase is not from Jesus. It's Nietzsche. Christians have swiped it for everything from web logs to one of Dr. Eugene Peterson's awesome books. Here is the long version:

"The essential thing in heaven and earth is a long obedience in the same direction; there results, and has always resulted in the long run, something which has made life worth living."

Christian ethics — belief in good, and action for the good — begins in self-denial and continues in … continuing. Forever and ever, amen. The Red Queen in *Alice's Adventures in Wonderland* puts it this way: "Begin at the beginning, continue until you get to the end, and then stop."

"A Christian ethic applied to all of life" is how we at Apologetics.com have said it on occasion. It affirms completely a consistency in living — in fact, it advocates it. It denies as fully the idea of compartmentalization — the nutty notion that we can put our faith in one place and our life in another. All things, sacred or secular, to the Christian, are the things of God: *The earth is the Lord's and everything in it.*

It helps here to remember faith is not a "leap in the dark" — something from part one, and associated with existentialism, which likes Nietzsche. Rather, faith is what we do — what we *do* — when evidence has already presented itself as a reliable resource. We place faith in that which has proved faithful, in that which is trustworthy.

Belief is not discrete, or separate from the rest of life, though it may be discreet: a quiet perseverance and consistency — a long obedience in the same direction.

Now there are other ways of living consistently. Quite obviously you can live consistently evil, and many people do. Between there and here are a number of options, and just as in the previous section duty compelled us to note reasonable opposing viewpoints (nothing compels a man to note unreasonable opposing viewpoints) we'll mention some here. Christians say, "deny self, live for God." Here's what others say:

"Please yourself." Sounds fun; ends in despair and death. Consider an Epicurean. Find that point where we get the most happiness. It's not the reckless, indiscriminate pursuit of any and all pleasure (that's a cousin of it called hedonism) but rather sort of the ultimate level of happiness, just *before* it starts to kill us.

In fact, you might even withhold a pleasure, to not ruin it for yourself. Eat a good meal but don't gorge yourself; have a drink with the buddies but don't end up vomiting in a strange bathroom.

Contemporary ethical egoism also relates to this. It's where we live for ourselves, only, but this is said to produce pleasure for all since we won't go "too far" — lest we harm ourselves. Right.

Overall it's self-centered or self-motivated — not necessarily in every regard *selfish*, as we would see that term, but surely revolving around personal experience.

Christians from Erasmus to John Piper have sought to work with ideas of ultimate pleasure by saying the greatest happiness is in a relationship with God, so there can be a Christian hedonism: they don't mean by this licentiousness, or least of all sin; it is perhaps a way of recapturing total ecstasy for the One who thought of it first.

Still, one major problem in this area is it leads to many immoral acts, when faced with personal pain, or possible death. A hedonist captured, tortured, and told to betray his country, friends, or family would do ... what? Exactly.

‡

"Don't please yourself." This may sound good, and may be part ways there, but there's no mention of God. This is stoicism. As far as it can go, it can go pretty far: arguing for detachment from things of the world and a stolid solidness of life. The stoic sees a bad thing, and it doesn't wreck his world. Unfortunately, the bad thing doesn't do *anything* to him, and neither does a good. The stoic's goal is to be impassive facing all.

This isn't Christianity. The Christian *weeps with those who weep*, and celebrates along with those who rejoice. The Christian is in the world but not of it, moving freely among men, carrying the message of God.

Stoicism is the art of becoming dispassionate: the polar opposite of the hedonist. Popularly speaking it can be similar to Buddhist ethics, though there are differences. It's detachment: hyper-independence from nearly anything — world peace receives the same response as world war. The stoic will be the one saying, "Whatever" — which means he isn't going to do anything.

Again, there's some value in this, and Christians have pursued a sort of stoicism in our monastic tradition, where strong attachments to the world are eschewed. Because God is the source of this here, you do get sometimes a better service, a more pure or complete ability to do some of the most powerful things in the universe: pray, for instance. But for most Christians, this is still not tenable.

‡

"A little of both," is syncretism. It's often thought of as incorporating the best of one thing (philosophy, say) with the best of another (religion). But what often happens in practice is you get neither.

Again isn't our Christian life all-encompassing? Can't we do *for us* and then do *for God*? Well, no.

Syncretism is like a hybrid car, where sometimes it runs on a battery and sometimes it's running on gasoline — but in any given moment we get the best of neither. You can't go as fast or as far or as fun. The parts rub against each other but they don't kiss, get married, and make love.

Some traditions in Christianity have tried this to a degree or another. We find a kind of Epicureanism in reformed churches, where the elect enjoy life, think wine and cigars. Meanwhile a Pentecostal church might bar such things altogether. There's a stoic beauty to Amish practice, and a stark simplicity in Quaker meetinghouses. Monastic practice continues.

But this is often just a way of saying, *Let's keep this part of life separate from this part of life*, and that's not ideal. The ideal is the full expression of all God has, transcending the incomplete mixtures of syncretism.

‡

"None of the above," is the judgment of ethical relativism — a word known to Christians to the point of being a bugaboo and a bogeyman, and a well-deserved one at that. It's a pretty thin perspective to say the least, not least of which because it is basically a negation: no one gets it right so everyone gets to do the thing they want.

Not only that, but it's right that they should do what they want. Whatever that means.

In fact, that's a way to think about ethical relativism: it's the disaffected youth, the immature adult, of ethics, offering the same word as stoics, in a different way: "Whatever."

The ethical relativist is the one saying, "Well, in their culture this is right, but in ours it's wrong." More simply: "True for you."

So if somebody wants to eat another human, OK. In fact, if you want to sell yourself *to be eaten*, that's also OK.

One big snag with ethical relativism is if a place says *ethical relativism* itself is wrong then it implodes in a burst of rationality. It's not just self-referentially false, but self-referentially absurd, to quote Ronald Nash.

And it happens that there is no place where it reigns. Boom.

‡

Consistency is often possible in non-Christian beliefs, in ways we act apart from God. We can practice evil continually (Romans says we do).

We can go for gusto and gustatory pleasures.

We can strip it down and live simply that others may simply live; we can a mix of these, adding, say a dash or peck to a form of faith.

We can pretend to dump it all as a means to behave any way we like.

Partial consistency is akin to saying "somewhat pregnant" or "mostly dead." Really, we want *consistent*, or let's just give up the program. These aren't words against incremental progress[18] but more saying, just do it. If we're going to *go for it* let's go for the Jesus of scripture and His example.

Looking out for number one

And what was that example?

It was Jesus washing the disciples' feet: this is where He says, literally, *I have left you an example, that you should do just as I have done to you.* This is John 13. Just twenty verses later, Jesus commands, *love one another, just as I have loved you.*

First, we deny ourselves.

Then, we do this in a life.

That is, we love God and others always.

We set aside our happiness to serve others. Lose our life to find it. We sacrifice completely, die daily, and surrender all.

Actually, this is one of Christianity's most convincing truths: that what we think leads to what we believe leads to what we do. It presents a fully orbed account of human life, giving specific counsel on what to do about it, wrapping it and overlapping it into this Christian faith. It's why many of us are apologists.

God is One and Jesus is God and we respond in obedience.

Obedience is self-denial, consistently, in a life of love.

Jesus Christ is the example. He consistently lived love and obedience to the One True God, with whom He exists in a never-ending dance of

---

[18] The Christian term is *progressive sanctification.*

deity. He's the source of our ethics, their reason and their aim. What we do (or don't!) in word or deed, we do all in the name of the Lord Jesus, by His power and for His good.

Christian ethics begins and ends with Jesus Christ

It can't but do so. *All things* begin and end with Jesus Christ.

One last thing: he set a new standard: not that we love others simply as we love ourselves, but that we love others *as Christ loved us*.

The greatest self-denial ...

The greatest pleasure ...

The greatest simplicity ...

The greatest integration ...

The greatest obedience ...

The greatest consistency ...

The greatest example ...

The greatest good ...

The greatest glory ...

All are in Jesus Christ.

We don't have to fully understand this, perhaps we never will, but we can start here and now, today. We needn't articulate it as a Platonic ideal, an Augustinian view, or Metho-Presbytero-Bapto belief.

Believe means we do it.

Under God to be sure, and only by the power of the Holy Spirit, we go for the grace "early and often" as voting was once done in Chicago. Then God's grace, God acting in our life to do what we can't do on our own, is bringing the life of love to fruition. The good tree bears good fruit.

We believe. So we act.

Chapter Three: An Excellent Pursuit

"How to be Good" — *that would be a cool title for a book.*

*Might not sell as well as one called "How to **Appear** Good" but it might do OK* — *if not, well … good.*

*We want to do it. It's worth it, since it shows we mean bidness with the truth claims. We know we don't **try** to be good: it's nothing but the blood of Jesus* — *and his teaching, that goodness is more about being than doing, and done as we become people who naturally do good, rather than futile attempts to try, try, try.*

And yet … and yet …

And yet, as we're becoming such people, we must, well … do. We pursue the weightier matters, while not neglecting these others — *the spices, or at least herbs, of life. We'll have a hundred chances this very day (perhaps we've had them already) to do good.*

*So what do we actually **do**?*

Introduction

Christians have talked about such things for nigh on 2,000 years. As long as there have been Christians we've discussed how to get that part of the equation right.

At the end of the last chapter, we started talking about it too. The good tree: how can it start bearing good fruit? We said we believe, then act.

We obey, therefore we are. Not exactly, but we can say *when* we obey, we are *truly*. Obedience is ineluctably linked to love: it actually is in the Scriptures, with a constant refrain of law + love, of loving God shown in adhering to his standards. Jesus affirms this, and says finally, simply, "If you love me, keep my commands." As C.S. Lewis put it from our side of the question, "I was not born free — I was born to adore and obey."

Go and do likewise.

Manna

What is it?

If we're to love and obey, what will it look like? We have many options but a classical answer to the question is love takes the form of excellence. Love is to "follow hard after" goodness and righteousness in oneself and for others. So when we obey, we are actually doing it.

This usually means virtue, more specifically *the* Virtues, those seven character traits, behaviors — actions — the Greeks started hashing out

---

Many Virtues

The four cardinal virtues (wisdom, justice, restraint, courage) were a "Golden Mean" between extremes of behavior. Courage, e.g., is between cowardly and foolhardy.

A second list is heavenly virtues, opposing seven deadly sins: chastity, temperance, charity, diligence, patience, kindness, and humility, attack lust, gluttony, greed, sloth, wrath, envy, and pride.

Meantime, seven holy virtues help pursue the good: courage, generosity, liberality, diligence, patience, kindness, and humility.

---

before the Incarnation, and the Church talked about

after, into its early centuries, until finally codifying them as a guide to life.

The seven: Prudence, Justice, Temperance, and Courage, Faith, Hope, and Charity. The first four are called *cardinal* because they came ... first, from the Greeks. The last three are *theological*, per Paul in 1 Corinthians.

Prudence is sometimes called Wisdom, Temperance can is thought of as Restraint, and Courage is sometimes known as Fortitude. Charity, of course, is better known as Love.

Virtues are the highest excellence, a pinnacle of human behavior. They are the Golden Mean[19] — the middle ground between two extremes. It's not compromise or average; a *mean* is the perfect balance of two choices, and thus it is the exactly right approach. When meals, celebrations, don't descend into gluttony or devolve into discussions of "meat and drink" ... we're in the neighborhood.

To some degree, the virtues are inseparable. Like the Fruit of the Spirit, stated singularly but as a long list ... is it several things, or one in parts? The virtues mutually connect always, though they're discernible as one at a time, and helpful to discuss separately.

Courage, C.S. Lewis reminded us, was needed to practice each of the other virtues, for instance, and an early pope, Gregory I, said there was no true wisdom that isn't also a just, temperate, and brave thing. Faith and hope tend to share travel expenses, as well, and love, of course, is the culmination of all acts.

Without it we're doing nothing but making a lot of noise.

The magnificent seven

Again: Prudence, Justice, Temperance, Courage, Faith, Hope, and Love.

Let's take a look at each of these more closely.

---

[19] The phrase is Aristotle's, from his *Nicomachean Ethics*.

Prudence or Wisdom … Now the fear of the Lord is the beginning of wisdom (Proverbs) but … what's wisdom? Fear of the Lord is a good piece of it, the beginning in fact. But wait, there is more.

Let's call it briefly the ability to choose between right and wrong. Clearly this is something that will require us to, as the old joke on how to get to Carnegie Hall goes, "Practice, boy practice." And if it's going to take awhile, best to get started. If we're not wiser at the end of our lives than we were at the beginning, there's going to be a problem — maybe even hell to pay. We'll be in "deep weeds" as one pastor we know is fond of noting.

Wisdom is so important there's a slew of books in the Bible we call "Wisdom Literature" — Ecclesiastes, Job, Song of Solomon, and, the King: Proverbs. Philosopher and author Peter Kreeft sees the first three of these as progressive: life as vanity, life as suffering, and life as love. Proverbs crowns them.

So: fear the Lord and read those four Old Testament books — a very good start.

‡

Justice has to do with knowing people should and shouldn't get and have and do, and what to do to help them get the first and not get the second, and what to do when they try to reverse it in practice.

For starters.

God's law teaches us justice, teaches us right-ness — what our forebears called righteousness — morally upright behavior that is … wait for it … virtuous.

"What does the Lord require of you: but to do justice, and to love mercy, and to walk humbly with your God?" (Micah 6)

‡

Temperance is at the least level, *restraint*. More strongly it is self-denial and self-sacrifice, and that's what we aim for. It's willingness to do without, to restrain or deny ourselves, for some greater good. Fasting is an obvious behavior, but it applies to more prosaic and practical — every day — behaviors, as well.

We might decline to defend ourselves when slandered, perhaps, or we might give up the comfort of a lazy Saturday at a movie or watching sports or even just meandering the mall, choosing instead to help a friend … do whatever. We're willing to act to our temporal detriment, for another's eternal, or at least greater, benefit.

What we give up isn't necessarily bad — in fact, it usually is neutral, as most things are. We don't give up food because we hate it; we give it up because we're giving that money for an effort at our church to provide food for others. So we fast, during lunch say, and we bring sandwiches to the homeless for that hour of the day.

Christ calls us to this, to the daily taking up of His cross — not just *the* cross, but *His* cross … which becomes *our* cross.

Courage + self-sacrifice is the essential context not only to make sense of the others, but simply to do them.

Oddly enough, another good word here is *balance*. What we've been saying doesn't sound like that, but remember that Mean: the "Golden Mean" the Virtues represent. We're striking the right balance between what we might want and what we should, in following Christ, do.

Over time those — what we want and what Christ asks — are going to come closer and closer together, and it won't seem a sacrifice at all.

‡

Courage is bravery; the old term is *fortitude*. Fear not. The ones who kill the body are nothing; no irredeemable harm comes to those who live in the Kingdom of God.

Remember Jesus in the boat, and the wind and the waves — which were about to obey Him, but just didn't know it yet! — crashed and slapped the boat around, while the disciples cowered? "Oh Lord, don't you even care about *us* — we're going to die!" God Incarnate coined a term for them on this occasion: You "Little Faiths" He called them. Get this. As He scolded them — even a little mockingly — for their fear, Jesus didn't mean they wouldn't die. He meant even if they died, what's to worry about?

That's courage.

Not, "God will keep me from dying."

But, "Even if I die, God will keep me."

Joseph, Moses, Joshua, David, Daniel … Jesus.

We will be called to courage in this life, have no fear.

‡

Faith is the inner inclination to believe what is true and to not believe what is false. Socrates — again with the Greeks, but after all … they started it — said if we say something is when it is, and isn't when it isn't, we're telling the truth. Faith is believing the truth: that what is, is, and that what is not … isn't.

It is not, mind you, "believing something on no evidence" or some other such canard. Biblically, faith is not opposed to *reason* — it is opposed to *sight*. We have faith our house or car isn't vandalized or vaporized or on fire, even though at present we can't see it. We believe someone is listening to us when we talk on the radio — we believe someone is talking to us when we listen to the radio!

A couple truths: there is a God, and He loves you.

A few falses: the evil or base or vile or destructive.

Without faith we can't please God. He exists, and He rewards those who diligently seek Him. Faith means understanding the truth.

‡

Hope is the certainty that, for instance, "He who began a good work" in us, will complete it. It's knowing there's an end to the beginning, and so we … begin. We start, and hope carries. We continue in sanctification because God has promised it will have results of perfection and completion.

Following Jesus is following Him to the cross — and it's damn hard work sometimes. It's not a holiday or vacation; it's not an errand or a nap. It's death, and it's going to tough. How much do you leave when you die? *You leave it all*, baby. Only we die *now*.

God is a god of hope. (Romans 15)

‡

Love is … well, it's the subject of an entire chapter in this part: the last chapter in the book. So without giving the ending away: know for now it's not a feeling, but rather what we actually do, though good feelings often come with actions. Love is *the will to good* — meaning if we love we're willing good things for someone (including ourselves), and we're going to do something about it. We're going to work at it.

Love is willing and working for the good.

Is it affection and warmth and tenderness and wool socks on a freezing morning? You betcha. But those come after we do it. Do not confuse them with the work; they are the results of it.

These are the seven — The Magnificent Seven. They are vital and virile ... they are life ... the virtues. They interdepend and they help one another grow and flourish like leaves on a tree, if you'll permit the cliché — it will make sense in a moment.

And something to remember, at least for our purposes here — the virtues as practiced by Christians have as their goal the continuing and continual presentation of our person to God so He will change us. We don't "do" the virtues to become super-cool; we do them to "present our bodies a living sacrifice" and to love God and love others. We do them to conform more and more to Jesus Christ, the "luminous Nazarene" and Lord of Creation and King of Galaxies past, present, and future.

And for one other, intensely practical purpose: to "give reason" for that hope in us, with "gentleness and reverence" before God, man, and whoever else might be watching. For the "good conscience" so the attacks on our Lord and King will *look* like the foolishness they *are*.

Placed in a Garden

Prudence, Justice, Temperance, Courage, Faith, Hope, and Love.

We asked earlier how a good tree begins bearing good fruit. This was neither *merely academic* (nothing is) nor rhetorical (few things are). The briefest answer at that time was: naturally. *You shall know them by their fruits*, said Jesus, in Matthew 7, speaking in context about prophets false and fair. It's agricultural wisdom for us all. The point of all this is when our actions come ... naturally.

Often, we needn't so much maim and kill our evil desires, though it may betimes be necessary to, take the Kingdom of Heaven by force. We might simply let dead branches die and ... fall off. We are *already* dead, remember, and we're being raised with Jesus Christ. Plan the work and work the plan as bidness guys say.

The *work out your salvation with fear and trembling, for it is God who works in you* approach of Philippians 2, is a good way to think on these things.

Cultivating a garden, raising vines, blooming flowers, or just growing a single tree to maturity, requires weeding, yes. But most time is spent making sure good stuff happens: good soil, air, sun, water ... maybe a little mulch or fertilizer ... and monitoring our little patch of heaven for signs of invasion, be it insect or plant. We note our Lord declined to root out the tares; maybe he knew something we don't.

So begin. Today. Now. Begin these virtues and what help you practice these virtues: prayer and study and silence and worship and fasting and celebration and solitude and service.

The very next thing you have to do, do what God wants. Then take the advice, again, of the King of Hearts: "Begin at the beginning, continue 'til you get to the end, then stop."

Adore and Obey

One final word.

Adore and obey.

Right: two words.

As you set this course, and we hope you will, for we all must — know this: we're apologists, folks are watching, and one day the master of the house will return. And this: it's not easy, but it gets easier. It's not easy, but it's easier than not doing it.

My yoke is easy, and my burden is light, and you will find rest for your souls, said Jesus. He told his disciples that even as they would be recognized by their love, they wouldn't be loved for it. They were painfully aware what happened to Jesus when he tried to love.

But there's no other way. Every other way fails. It's frustrating, awful, and we hope you don't know what we mean here but you do; we all do. To say it plainly, every other way is lukewarm spit.

"How long will you go limping between two different opinions," asks the good, and so-human prophet Elijah. "If the Lord is God, follow Him; but if Baal, then follow him." (1 Kings 18)

The text goes on, "And the people did not answer him a word."

We have a word for them, and for you — two in fact.

Adore and obey.

(There's no other way.)

Chapter Four: What Shall We Do

We were talking of the Seven Virtues: Prudence, Justice, Temperance, Courage, Faith, Hope, and Love. Wisdom and rightness, and self-sacrifice, and just plain, old-fashioned guts. Adore and obey, was in there, too.

Well, the best laid plans of mice and men …

Because sometimes it doesn't work as we planned. As "The Princess Bride" puts it, "You keep saying that word. I don't think that word means what you think it means."

*Talking is good and planning may be essential, but **Are we doing?** is crucial.*

- *Be holy in all you do … do good (Peter)*
- *Be doers of the Word … not only hearers (James)*
- *His commands … His word … walk as he walked (John)*
- *Hold fast to what is good … outdo one another (Paul)*

Or this from Christ: "If you love me, you will keep my commands."

Indeed.

Introduction

One author asks it this way:

Are we merely, "a featherless biped?"

Or is man much more: "a little less than God?"

This is from *Run With the Horses*, about the life of the prophet Jeremiah. Eugene Peterson is quoting Cleanth Brooks,

"One looks for an image of man attempting in a world increasingly dehumanized to realize himself as a man — to act like a responsible moral being, not to drift like a mere thing."

Of course this goes for women too: "man" here is not to offend, but to classify, to separate: people are neither cabbages nor kittens. We are free to, well … adore and obey.

Images of God

Scripture answers the question — "biped or titan?" — this way:

"The second one."

It says we're "a little lower than the angels." That's the English from the Septuagint, the Greek Old Testament. A translation might also say, "a little lower than God," says our ESV notes. We read Psalm 8:5, "*You* have made them" that way. *God* made us just below those angels. "*He* crowns us with glory and honor" and "*He* gives us the dominion" over *His* creation. It keeps the order right — while showing us what people should, and can, strive for. The praise goes to *Him*. (Psalm 8:9)

The last chapter was about what we should do. Here we say we *can* do it, and why. When we talk about love and virtue and when we set out to begin, we have a place to stand, and we can move the world[20]. By God, we are slightly lower than God;

> **The Main Thing**
>
> It's easy to get lost in abstraction when talking about the virtues, easy when speaking of love, and we're talking about both. As management gurus say, "The main thing is to keep the main thing the main thing."
>
> First: Men and women bear the image of God. We can and must be good.
>
> Second: Being good *is* personal: "Love your neighbor."
>
> Third: Others don't always want love. Pray and prepare for a day they do.

---

[20] Archimedes said that.

with this divine mandate, and the tools he provides, we can "do this thing" now.

And the primary tool is himself.

Because scripture also says we're all made in the image of God.

Even before we get to the part about *a little lower than* God, we're told we share in His nature. Not the big stuff but shadows of all of it, and many cool things besides.

That we can stems from who we are in God: created for eternity, as a rational, moral being, who can know himself and God, the difference between good and evil, and who can do something about all this. More than molecules in motion, more than a mere catalog of parts, or spare parts, in some thought, man is amazing to behold. Hamlet ends on a down note about the whole enterprise, but begins by acknowledging,

> *"What a piece of work is a man! How noble in*
> *reason? How infinite in faculty? In form and moving*
> *how express and admirable? In action how like an angel?*
> *In apprehension, how like a God? The beauty of the*
> *world. The paragon of animals ... "* − Act 2, Scene 2

There's something wonderful about us, and it's an essential human dignity, irrepressible and undeniable — and obvious, for those with an ear to hear or an eye to see. As some would redesign us by technology or dehumanize us through ads or slogans or suppress us by force of law ... it will not hold.

Unless we let it do so.

Yeats lamented "the best lack all conviction, and the worst are full of passionate intensity." Such evil can only triumph, said Jefferson, when good men do nothing.

The battle is the Lord's and it's time to join in. We can do it, we have been created to do it, and in good conscience we must do it.

Why we should stems from the same source. Our *imago Dei* gives us the ability, and the confidence in that ability, to begin and continue — and finish. The first reason we should is based on the same fact: a planet full of God's images needs us.

"What are we — this world — waiting for?"

It is waiting for Christ-formed people to fulfill our call in the world he sets before us daily, people *he* sets before us daily. Tim Gautreaux writes in one of his stories that when good people *won't* do the right thing, we leave a void soon filled by evil people who *will* do it.

People have the image of God.

They have inherent human dignity.

They need us. They need you.

Will it "work" … will we succeed at being good? Yes, we will succeed. But it's not our concern. Because we remember: the battle isn't ours … it's *his*. Or as T.S. Eliot says, "For us there is only the trying. The rest is not our business."

All Polity is Personal

It may not shock you to know the word "politics" and the word "polite" do *not* share the same development. Back in the pre-Christian Athenian day they may have had the same basic root: *polis,* or "city."

But by 1500s, though both words are about relationships with people — being *civil* in a corporate or an individual sense — the personal one, *polite,* gets help from a new word meaning "to polish."

Maybe related, a few differences ... but boy do we mess them up.

We remember, sometimes, that God said, somewhere, how people are made in the image of, well ... him. His people, he made, in his image.

But when the rubber meets the road, we forget. We get into life and it gets confusing, at least busy. We forget, is the long and short of it.

And when the conversations start, we really forget.

Political debates, theological discussions, basic personal exchanges ... and the "image of God" part escapes us as we pursue ... something. We don't *do* image at the moment. We might even be right, but no, it doesn't matter: we'd do the same things if we weren't right, stepping on people on our way to the top of the winning heap.

A personal interaction with friend, family, co-worker, or even stranger in our midst, becomes another chance to give our side, say our piece, and ... get it right.

Or we go another way: we want to address that world issue or end this world problem or just comment on someone's blog. We think our view is essential to the discussion. As an infamous cartoon, viral on the web, of course, shows it: when someone asks if we have to respond *right now*, we say, "Yes, we do! Someone is wrong on the Internet!"

Sheesh. What we'll trade for love. What won't we!? What we will trade for a simple obedience to God's call. Pursuing *politics* we forget *polite*.

It does no good if we win an argument and hate our brothers.

It does no good if we seek tit-for-tat word trading, above care.

It does no good to be the tinkling cymbals and clanging gongs.

And our job is to do good.

We are in the image of God; so are they. God's image borne is lived by *the one, true, God* who gave us his image, and who gave it to all others, as well. And the interaction of all three — our image, theirs, and God who made us both — must lead us to focus on the two in that list who aren't us: God and others.

We're pursuing abstraction, a big picture, and forgetting the strangers at our gates, or even the neighbor at the door.

Here is how to begin.

See every person as one. Presume we are personal beings who will live eternally: we have never met a mere mortal, says C.S. Lewis. So see them as such: eternal. There is no one like us, and no one like *them*. A human is personal, rational, emotional, and able to think in terms of good and evil; this separates us from everything in the universe.

That woman, one pew over, *Christ died for her.*

That man, who just cut you off, *Christ died for him.*

We are the children of our heavenly father. That's what we *are*. We're not an accidental accumulation of atoms. We have meaning and we have purpose: that is part of our essence. We're not essentially of one position or another, one party or another, one people or another. We are men and women, billions and billions of them, made in the image of God.

We express that purpose by loving our neighbors as ourselves.

We love those men and women as Christ loved them: one at a time.

All polity is personal. It means when we set out to practice the virtues, to love God and others, we drop the pretense — including that given us, perhaps without our knowing, by party, place, or people. As important as those may be in their times, the daily *what-do-we-do-now?* is about reflecting the image of God — the intensely personal being of the Father, the Son, and the Holy Spirit.

Our life is more than a "Mean People Suck" bumper sticker.

That obedience is what we were made for, who we are, and who we are affirmed to be in Christ. We're to treat others, each individual other, with dignity and care and love — not incidentally, the same as Christ did for us, in His life and death and resurrection. We're for loving our neighbors. Some have even said we're for loving our enemy.

We must be *more* concerned with loving our neighbor than with what the President, or even the pastor, is or isn't doing. Doesn't mean we are not concerned at all, or even that the life God gives us ought to be used to keep tabs on them. It might be our job and it is certainly a duty.

It is simply to say, that is *not* the most important thing. When we speak with the tongues of men and angels and have not love, it's nothing ... so it doesn't matter if we speak *to* presidents and prime ministers, or voters and viscounts, pastors and presbyters. Have not love? ... zip.

(We keep coming to love ... we'll come back to it fully, we promise.)

Indirection

Everyone thinks of changing humanity but no one thinks of changing himself[21].

Now that we're thinking of it, and thinking of it in terms of one single life, there is one more thing to say. Don't try it.

Don't try to be good.

But ... but ... what about everything we've said?

---

[21] Tolstoy said that

Heck — what about everything the Bible says?

- Colossians 3 — "elect of God ... put on tender mercies, kindness, humility, meekness, patience ... forgiving one another"
- Romans 12 — "Bless those who persecute you ... rejoice ... weep ... live in harmony ... associate with the lowly ... repay no one evil ... do what is honorable ... live peaceably with all."

What about dozens of passages that tell us to *do things*?

What about "love your enemy" — what about that one?

Yes, of course. This is what to do.

What we mean is, don't try to be good as the means of doing good. Of course we try, every moment we can — we try with every person every day every time.

We mean don't *only* try, or even *mainly* try. Remember: indirection. As we don't simply talk about it, but do it, so we don't do it, but become the kind of person who naturally does it ... *Words, words, words — I'm so sick of words*[22].

Indeed. Many people are sick of words, and quite a few are sick even of watching what we do — even when we do it right.

They'll know we're Christians by our love, but they don't always like it. It is much an affront and offense to them as the cross itself. Sometimes people don't want anything done: the thing looks like it's being done *to* them instead of *for* them. They may be mistaken. We know. Indirection.

Do three things:

- *Praying for them, for us, for all.* This is the most powerful thing we can do. We know you've heard that before. We can't make you know it in

---

[22] Eliza Doolittle said that, in "My Fair Lady."

your marrow, in the capillary tips of the fingers and toes — but that's how we feel it, in our best, most loving moments. If we had to choose between praying and doing we would pray.

• *Doing what we can.* Most commonly we needn't make those choices. We can both pray and do. Then pray more, if a moment presents itself, or even if it doesn't. It's a classic Christian formulation: *pray and work.* It hearkens back centuries and is the key for us now.

• *Preparing for more.* This is where we think — see part one for a good start — and plan. This is in the quiet of our rooms and the communion of our churches. It is in disciplines like solitude and silence and study, and fasting and feasting and service. We make ourselves ready to do good, when God will give the chance. We put ourselves, daily, more than daily, before him, so we won't miss a one.

And of course we pray for such times. And do it when they come.

Station Break: Eloquent Acts

*Apologetics is not complete **until** we act.*

The story thus far: we've got really good reasons for thinking as Christians. Jesus is Lord and he rose from the dead. Scripture is reliable. We have logical reasons and compelling evidence for all this. We think, think, and think more.

*That's where we began: believers **thinking**. But, it the book **is** about **believers** thinking. It's about people who **believe**, that is to say … **act**.*

We must live it out: work out salvation, unto godliness, and being holy. Holy, godly exercise and work. Exercise. You'd be surprised how much the ADC staff

enjoys its mixed martial arts! Think of ethics and virtue as MMA for real life —
only without the tattoos and blood.

Sometimes there's blood.

There was the first time.

What we're aiming for is a **vibrant** and **muscular** life. The vibrancy is virile
thought: hard work on the life of the mind. The muscularity is virtuous action:
hard work in a life lived in bodies.

Virile minds in virtuous bodies — there should be a Latin phrase for that. We
could start our own shoe company and use it as the name.

So now we've discussed God's idea of good, what that means for our behavior,
and how to begin. So begin, already.

If we get one or two of us doing it, we could start a club, with handshakes and
a tree house and stuff. We don't want to say what might happen when we get
more than one or two of us doing it.

We might even change the world. There's precedent for it.

OK, I'll tell you. If a whole bunch of us got together, maybe in a church or I
dunno ... go nuts with it. Say we started, sometimes, **doing** some of the things
we only talk about, or kept doing them once we do start. Because, to be honest,
we sometimes get it right, do pretty good and all. We could just maybe world-
change. Or something.

Chapter Five: God, Men, Law

Think Bilbo.

*Can't just go **there**. Has to come **back again**. Can't just get ourselves going, committed — tanned, rested, ready, willing, and able. Because as soon as we do people are going to get uncomfortable. If they didn't like us when we weren't a loving bunch of crazy Christians, what will they do when we are?*

It's our job betimes — to afflict the comfortable, while comforting the afflicted — but it ain't no fun when we actually get down to it. They misunderestimated our resolve, and now we're in the middle of loving them, and they go,

*"Whoa! Hold on there! Where's the fire! What **is** going **on** here?"*

C.S. Lewis says we object lustily (pardon the expression) when God starts his total reclamation project of us. We thought it'd just be a coat of paint, and some Bondo® ... new curtains ... shelves in the garage, if the Lord feels energetic.

Did we think it'd be easier to bring the Law of the Lord to bear on societies?

Introduction

World changing and culture making are not for the faint of heart.

That's the truth, if you really want to know it.

Sorry to say something as obvious as a prom night pimple, but people will not like it when we start *working out our salvation* in their immediate presence or if we sweat like a prodigal son's pigs with our *exercising unto godliness.*

And leave us not even start on *being we holy.*

Love writ large threatens. You will be accused of all manner of evil:
like we want a theocracy, or we're a bunch of crackpots, or we really,
truly, deeply hate all of them.

It's Like This

One of the staff apologists here knows a guy named Charlie. They see
each other sometimes at a Starbucks. Charlie nurses a single cup of
coffee for hours: he has nowhere to be and doesn't need to be there any
particular time. He seems to have no teeth, but our apologist is not
sure.

Then again he might because Charlie loves chocolate chip cookies. Of
this our apologist is certain, as he has bought him several of these. The
team member can't be sure what it does for his heart, but it sure does
make Charlie smile. They're friends.

When we seek to make this sort of personal interaction something a
society can do — whatever form it might take, we're not trying to say
here — that's when it gets even harder than we thought it might be,
trying to make friends with Charlie.

Oh, right.

They already say that.

God

A quirky thing happens these days, though it happened in others too.

When we try doing what God wants, we're theocratic crackpot haters.
So we dial it down, and learn people want … lots of things he wants.

OK, they don't want it because God wants it, and they don't want God
at all, and that's why the various plans and schemes out there go south
for all remaining winters.

But they say they want it, and some even pursue that desiccated, God-
absent version, and the fact remains, most of what Christians say to do is
what they demand of us, right after the complain about us saying it.

It has ever been thus: we're accused of holding up an impossible standard. And we're excoriated for not meeting it. This, to say the least, does not seem fair, and not much has changed.

God calls us to Him. We begin to follow. We see His counsel is good for others, too. We start charities, hospitals, ministries, and the like, to bring these ideas even further into society's life. Then we realize it would go faster if other people got on board.

They say butt out ... we roll with that, turn the other cheek ... and watch them try to do the same things, but without God. Maybe they get a government involved — but government (honest) is not God.

No, no, no, we say. You have to do it like *this*.

Now they're really ticked.

Well, the truth is ... no, no, no. We did it wrong. Still do.

We focus on what people are *doing*. We see all the ways our lives are changed and truly want them to change theirs. We're doing stuff — and we know they can do stuff, too.

God bless any inch of earth where Christ-formed people work to make life better. Heaven help 'em all and may their tribes increase.

But it starts with God.

That's where it started with us, and that's where it has to start with anyone else. Yes, yes — salt and light ... shine before men ... that they may know. We vote for all those.

But it's not about voting.

But don't skip the part about God. Don't let's make it just some pretty words. Maybe church should be 25 minutes of Holy Communion and prayer, and six minutes of sermon, 'stead of the other way. Sometimes?

Salt and light …

Shine before men … so they see God's glory.

That they may know … and also want to change their lives.

Seek we third the Kingdom of God? No, no, no. Seek we first. God surely wants what He wants. Not terribly controversial, that idea. But what He wants *first* is *us*. People. Our hearts.

As alluded to in the previous chapter, so we say here: God first.

Remember all this was His idea. Whatever we do well, whatever is good and true and beautiful … it was His idea. When we turn out attentions to others, as we will here in a moment, remember C.S. Lewis' literary mentor, George MacDonald, on our goal for others: "I want you to grow as beautiful as God intended, when He thought of you first."

Remember too, and finally, and again — they won't be happy about this. It needs to be said more often, as Christ said it often when He was here: they'll know who we are by our love but they themselves will love darkness rather than light. They will

> ### Anyway
> With more than a few reservations about cowboy hats on non-horsemen and coiffed crooners where once we had disreputable whiskey drinkers and guys who'd done time … *do it anyway.*

scream and rail and fight. They may even kill us and think they're serving God.

Some want a kingdom, as one might sing, but they don't God in it.

That makes all the difference.

And Man

Now ... we don't always get this right.

In many ways, we fail.

In chapter four of this part, this section on how we Christians must act ... do ... live, we said Remember! It starts with each one, the individual: that is, with every *one* of us.

Now we're talking not just about each of us but about all of us: all people in society and nation; state or commonwealth; county, city, neighborhood, block, street.

It does indeed start with each of us. As Tolstoy said, "Everyone thinks of changing humanity, no one thinks of changing himself." The lesson there, of course is to think of changing oneself before getting our crazy on and bounding off in all directions. It says further that *the way* to change humanity is to change us.

But changing humanity *is* in there. It's part of the *dealio*: the full picture isn't full without out.

So we started this book with Jesus, and everything, every *thing*, we think flows from Him. We started this section with what God wants — His *ethics*, as is said. Every belief (meaning, every action) flows from that. Personally, our pursuit of goodness is about the image of God in us, the Christ of God before us, the Spirit of God leading us.

And so we act, because now we truly can.

Not just *we're able*, but with that foundation — one regularly and conscientiously renewed every day, and as many times a day as needed — we have a shot at getting it right, at "doing something" for God.

Consider some of the best things we've done — starting charities, ending evils, work in political and economic practices — and God shall be at the start of it, God will be at the heart of it. If it's lasted a thousand years, we didn't do it. He did. In fact it's a feature of incredible accomplishment that it's incommensurate with the ability of the humans involved to have done it.

When we work for God among people, it must be work *for God* first. When we fail, it's because it wasn't — because He wasn't. We want to extend the changes God has wrought in us personally to all people, or at least more of them, but, as Eugene Peterson notes, we try to bring the *Truth* and the *Life* in the wrong *Way*:

- We're pushy. We think being right is most important — sometimes more important than doing some small good; too often more crucial than love. We know, well we sort recall, there's nothing greater than love, but we keep ... it ... up. Pushing. 'Til we've knocked 'em down or they're pushing back or they've knocked us down, or all three.

- We get bogged on details. Specific ways of implementing, some of 'em important and some of which aren't. Some of the details are also theological, resurrecting that old charge of "Theocracy!"

- We give up. This is the worst result of all. It may be we should slow down or back off entirely (if we're pushy), or refocus and start over (if we're bogged down) but we never should quit.

We lose focus. We shift the focus to who (meaning *us*), or shift the focus to how (meaning the way *we* want it), or shift the focus to, well, *us* again, meaning we're taking our marbles and going home, if we haven't lost all of them by then, that is.

You know what we're going to say here.

You know where our focus should be.

Each day, as many times daily as needed, we return. In sin and sorrow, failure and forgetting, pain and planning, we begin again, and again, and again.

We show.

We teach.

We live it.

If we keep this up, we just might get something done around here.

In the Public Square

Deep breath …

This is how Christians do it, how we used to do it, and truly how we sometimes manage to do it today. It's how we can do it again.

We apply God's thoughts to challenging problems at amazing levels — millions or more may benefit, we believe! We *believe.*

We seek to influence society (people) and culture (what they do) in vast and numerous ways. We aim more for a sand-on-the-shore or a leaven-in-the-lump approach rather than a "Mongol hordes" method, but inexorably, ineluctably … we do it.

We remain confident and humble — that most difficult of pairings. We say these things we as people, as *a* people, *must* do. We do them. We say to work for the virtues, and then we actually do work for them.

We march, or sit-in, or stand up, or serve and stand and wait, in what the late Richard John Neuhaus called The Public Square. He made this phrase the clarion for Christian effort on behalf of the *polis.* John Snyder, a former host of the Apologetic.com radio show, works with the ideas it suggests, as well.

The idea it suggests for our purposes is there is a place to *do* on a grand scale. There are issues to address, projects to plan, and problems to solve.

There is work to be done, and we're to do it.

But remember. Remember. Remember the good tree and good fruit. Don't mistake what can be done with changed minds and hearts: the thought and action, to connect it to the present book.

Work like nuts, yes. But changed hearts is God's top goal. Good fruit come only from good trees and good trees come only from God.

A distinct danger for Christians, for anyone, is to get behind something and want it more than why we got behind it: valuing the vessel over the treasure. Then it's a short trip, and fall, to thinking anyone *not* on board with it, must be … dealt with. At that point *losing focus* would be swell, compared to what such people are about to do.

There are two norms: first is the civil norm of the law, where we spec out what human laws should be by God's moral law. The second norm is the ideal and ultimate perfection God requires of us. We pursue the first in The Public Square, because the second only comes by God's grace and the heart of one who is his.

Changed hearts is his number one goal.

Further, we find our ultimate everything in God because he's the only One big enough to hold it all. So we never expect the fruit of relationship with God to come even from moral law enacted in society. Don't expect human methods, let alone human goals, to produce what God alone can do.

Only God can make good trees.

Our lives are to be an expression of him. But it's only possible *by* him. It's a great act of moral clarity to sacrifice for others (it is belief) and it's a great act of moral clarity to reason clearly (it is thinking). But these stand eternally only *in* him.

Now clearly Christ taught moral law. You can't read ten lines of Jesus speaking, let alone the entire Sermon on the Mount, without seeing he's bringing God's ways to large swaths of people. In neighborhood or city or nation — hillsides or villages or provinces — as well as the cranking huge metropolis of Jerusalem, we'd add: a burg giving up no ground on diversity, cosmopolitanism, or the messiness of humanity in its day, to a London or Paris or New York City, in ours.

But Jesus is going deeper. He talks the Kingdom of God and you know he's got something big in mind. With anything God's Son says and does we know that. He wants more.

Not just moral law, but eternal life.

Not just what we do, but all we are.

So when we're building a society, yes, we're setting up systems. We're working out laws — do this, don't do that — and what happens if we do and what happens if we don't. We build our *civitas* on this law, and hold people accountable to that.

But Jesus' moral outline is more exacting and deeper, and it cuts to the quick. Is it mercy or justice? Sorry, it's quite harder. It's both.

God's law is perpetual, and must be worked out in practice.

So.

Go forth.

Think.

Write.

Speak.

Augustine said it thus:

Love, and do what you will.

Chapter Six: Only Natural

Love and do what we will.

Sounds dangerous. Love is.

That Augustine was a firebrand, you know: a rabble-rouser. A troublemaker if you want to know the truth. Told the truth, he did, even when it made him look bad. Told it more, especially when it made the devil look bad.

Told it yet more, and we came to understand more of what makes God so good. Oh that Augie.

So it sounds dangerous to say Love, and do what you will.

Because it is dangerous to say Love, and do what you will.

Because if we tell people, **do what you will** *... what will they do? We can't know and, on top of* that, *we tell them to* **love***. Talk about danger. Can we take the risk, especially when we're out there changing the world?*

Introduction

So it turns out you **can** legislate morality.

In fact, we do nothing else.

Our every act is a statement.

It's an example, an instantiation, as the philosophers say, of what we believe (belief is action) about how life should be, how it actually is. It's how we'd live if we had our druthers, and it often is. It's how we'd vote if we ran the circus, and it often is.

A circus ... *and* how we vote. How much more is it the case when we do vote or speak or, as God calls us to do so, promote and pass laws, or make public policy?

The real question is: how will we do it? Will we legislate the morality, well … morally … or one of the other ways? Once an obvious answer rises, how do we do it?

Reality

We do it naturally.

We do it via natural law[23].

Natural law means even a border collie knows what to do. Heck, even a basset hound knows. These are foundational elements that, when we're connected with them, all the details — the down-and-dirty practicals, the organizing, caucusing, campaigning, voting — will come … naturally.

Natural law is real.

It's the really real.

The real. The *real*.

Reality is what is, whether we want it, like it, agree with it, vote for it, or not. Reality is what is (or isn't what isn't) whether we even know it or not. Probably not a controversial concept if you've read in part one, but lots of people, but probably not as many as the newspapers tend to say, believe (act on) odd things, regarding the real.

Other people have ethics, and they're not all Christians.

Also not controversial but it has effects. One effect is a fact: others treat people differently based on their ethics, and not always, need it be said,

---

[23] *Natural* isn't always OK. We work in and on a fallen creation, and man in his *natural* state may mean living at a level of base, animal instincts — our urges. Not good. But *natural* in the good sense means **things acting in accord with the order for which they were created.** This is the idea that it takes more than being common, or, on an even weaker level, what is simply *now the case*, to be natural. Natural Law, then are the laws of reality — the way life as God created it *is*, whatever it looks like at the time to us, and will be again, *when things act in accord with the order for which they were created.*

in horrible ways. It's not like we have a lock on ideas for being good. We need to make sense of that. How is it done? What does it mean for us, or society, and Christians active for change in our country and world.

We're not being facetious. We're preparing to ask honestly — *Are we imposing* (we'll use that word people use) *our ethical ideas on others? Are we forcing scads of people to do what we "happen" to think best?*

It's a common accusation and we must learn to hear and respond to it. The short answer is no.

A slightly longer answer is that it isn't what we *happen* to think best ... and we don't force any to do it, any more than any other law in ... force. As if we could.

We base everything on God, but we base a good deal of our effort and the reason for it, on natural law. Which itself is based on God, but that's for another time. The truth is, most people, for most times, in most places have thought certain things were objective: they were just ... *there* ... no matter if we wanted or liked, agreed with or voted for — or even knew about it.

Murder, slavery, murder and slavery, poisoning the parakeets, kicking babies for fun: sure some people disagreed (some people still do) but the majority believe these are bad, no matter how much they may wish you could own another person and order them around all the time, and then kill them when you got bored.

Even on the "lesser" levels — lying, cheating, stealing, cursing, all the way "down" to spitting on the sidewalk, and cracking your knuckles in public — there is strong consensus.

Even when we don't do these things, we feel the need to give the *very good reasons* why *in this special case* we *were justified in doing it.* In other words, even when we *fail* to do the agreed-upon acts, we know we *should have* done it, and we have to explain *why we didn't.*

That's natural law.

Life, liberty, etc.

Happiness (and the pursuit thereof) … rights (and duties) … oughts and can'ts and must-do-its … natural law.

Sorry.

But … someone will say … that is *not* natural law. It's just the social contract, it's just an agreement between people because we have to live together and not stab each other in the back, or even in the front for that matter. So I agree not to steal your stuff, then you agree not to steal my stuff. It's an extension of the Golden Rule.

Yeah! We say. Yeah — the Golden Rule: it's just doing unto others as we'd have them do unto us. Thomas Hobbes had a social contract idea and so did Jean Jacques Rousseau. Even John Locke had one, and wasn't he a favorite of our Founding Fathers?

It's a discussion we might also have to have.

Later.

Suffice to say for now this isn't the picture in scripture. It's not what we see from God, who in the beginning existed before man and nary a word there is about a "state of nature."

Rather God's exact moral nature is expressed in all he does: in creating things, including man. More than just including man, because man is His highest creation and among other things, one thing most clearly expressed there is ... natural law.

Sorry.

We're back to knowing it's wrong to kill, lie, cheat, steal.

Such ideas have been considered objectively true since Plato, on down through centuries by Augustine, Aquinas, Luther, Calvin, and coming into U.S. history, Jonathan Edwards, Charles Hodge, and others. From the beginning until now, men have believed God gave man a nature. So certain acts were either for man or not for man, as they did or did not do (fulfill) his ultimate purpose in God.

Human flourishing is the end measure of natural law.

‡

But, someone will say, study different cultures and some of them are horrific — they each other ... kill old people ... have sex with children.

Yes, we patiently respond: they don't live in accord with natural law. Those cultures could use a liberal dose of infused Christianity, to make, transform, that culture and bring it closer to understanding reason, and relationships, and community, and law: natural law.

‡

But, someone will say, you're trying to put us under the law. Even a few Christians will say, you're trying to make us do according to some ancient texts that don't even apply anymore.

Well, we patiently respond: guess what? You're already under law, the law, whether you know it or not. Not murdering, not slaving, not ... you call it ... is an expression of what it is to be in God's image — we don't murder because the other person is in the image of God ... that is *why* you don't want to do it. It's God's moral nature, given before we got here in Natural Law, and it's never going to change.

‡

But, someone will say (someone always says it), that's all fine, all good, want-like-agree-vote for it — but how do you *know* it is the natural law? How do we know this particular thing is truly natural — that is, the way things should act in accord with the order for which they were created?

That's fine.

We can have that discussion. We want that discussion. We would love to have that discussion. Because at least we now agree: there is a natural law.

God created man in knowledge and original righteousness, able to tell truth from life and good from evil — so in and from the beginning there has been … natural law.

There's been a relationship of love, and in the breakdown of that love, society breaks down too. Which gives us a second foundational element: one is natural law, and the other is love.

Love

Again we see the foundation of everything is love.

Specifically here, the foundation of *law* is love.

The fulfilling of the law is to love God and love your neighbor, and that includes when we're trying to effect societal change, and it includes when they disagree with us, when they think we're being those theocratic loonies, when they don't get the whole virtues thing, when they've certainly never heard of Natural Law — and by the darn way, it won't work to confuse the issue, and stop trying to change the subject when the truth is you guys are just really, really mean.

Whew.

It's a hard road.

It's a tough way to live.

But what other way is there?

To live, that is — to truly live?

They will say natural law is ambiguous, nebulous, and confusing — and we mean they'll say it after you do all the work in the first part of this chapter.

And you will have to nod and smile and start over ... with love.

And it's not about affection or self-fulfillment — and you knew that, but in this case we mean it's not about *your* affection for them (or theirs for you) or whether *you* will be self-fulfilled by talking, more and more and more, about this.

We don't legislate according to affection and fulfillment: it's according to natural law. And natural law works says it according to how it fits the order God made.

We don't make laws in different ways (red means stop no matter what we say of God) though we make them for different reasons.

We make them for love.

Not love as personal desire, not love as feeling, but love as the highest good for society, and thus, for each individual, each person ... each one.

A few chapters back we discussed three ideas for moving forward in belief — that is, in action — and actually how to do it. Think of it as a personal ethic. It was, of course, based on love.

Corporate ethical efforts are based on the same thing: love. It matters little to us (or reality, for that matter) whether the changes are for one or one million ... or 310 million in the U.S., according to the most recent Census figures.

Now this presupposes you've read chapter four of this section.

Once you have, you'll know: first we love them.

Once we settle on that, here's how:

• *Pray for them.* If they are our enemies, we pray for them ... more. So, *Bless my enemies O Lord, even I bless them, and do not curse them.* So pray. We're praying without ceasing anyway (1 Thessalonians 5), so we can toss some prayers in for those we know.

• *Do for them.* We find ways to serve and care for those we know, and even who we don't. We wow them with concern and ... actually doing it. People in our neighborhood, the guy we see at the copier at work or our kids' teachers. In line at the grocery store or the voting booth. We mean to say: the people with whom we're forming this society of ours.

• *Prepare for them.* Why doesn't this come before Do? Why not first? So we can act *now* and fill the needs we see now ... then prepare for more and greater and other wonderful ways we will wow them tomorrow.

And also because we *always* pray first, right after love, and sometimes at the same time.

Chapter Seven: Love

It was the Winter of Love.

An apologetic.com staffer once taught Sunday school, ending with a session on love. It consisted of all the verses in the entire Bible with the word "love" in them. All the verses, in the entire Bible, that included the word love. Every one of the verses, in both the Old and New Testaments, that mentioned love, in any form, whatsoever.

There was no direct teaching, and quite a learning experience; his wife called the entire series, culminating with all those verses, "The Summer of Love." He couldn't call it anything, the staffer, because he couldn't say a word through all the tears.

Do a key word search on love. Some of us like the ESV website — there's even an app for it — but Bible Gateway or something similar works fine. Search.

Then read all the verses. Out loud.

No, some don't fit. But if you aren't bawling by Joshua, congrats: you're a Cyborg.

And trying to make it through the Psalms? No way.

Way.

Introduction

We are People of The Book — The Love Book.

We talk with some justification about 1 Corinthians 13 being the love chapter, but in the end we're more partial to Romans 12, especially the last 12 verses. *Pshaw!* to the whole idea of a love *chapter*.

The Bible is the Love *Book*. We don' need no stinkin' chapters.

And trying again to make it through the Psalms? No way.

Way.

Course He's Not Safe

Love is dangerous, we said. Love and do what you will, we said.

There's only one way this works, only one way it's not dangerous.

Jesus Christ.

Oh ... wait. Our bad. It's still dangerous.

C.S. Lewis again:

"But is He safe?" Lucy asks.

"'Course He's not safe!" say her Narnian friends — but He's good.

One of the first dangerous things we learn is you can't just not "smoke or drink or go with girls who do" when trying to love and obey. If that is or was ever enough, we could date the dog, who probably doesn't smoke or drink. Depends on the dog. Maybe ones in North Carolina ...

In other words, we can't be satisfied simply with behavior or negative commands (thou shalt nots) and the like.

God wants more.

With love, He doesn't just want a kid to stop hitting his brother. He says, "Love your brother." It's harder and easier, but it's the only real law there is, we're told, so we've got to get cracking.

We're told to love our neighbor, and then Jesus says not to ask who our neighbor is, but who can we be neighbors to — and the answer to *that* is of course as boundless and never-ending as God Himself.

It's not true that love asks for nothing. Sometimes it asks all.

Including our lives if necessary.

That's dangerous.

But God sends His Son to show us how it's done, and how it'll all be OK, alright to die at first, to die to self, to die to our desires for the sake of others, and to ask them to die to theirs for still more others. It will be painful at first: recall the lizard that is lust in Lewis' *The Great Divorce*, and oh, how it screamed when the fiery angel broke its back!

It hurt the man to do it, but the angel didn't say it wouldn't.

Then again, God doesn't promise to keep us from dying.

He promises that if we die He will keep us.

See what we mean?

Dangerous.

Love and Live for God

A confession …

In one sense we could have skipped the first 14 chapters, posted this as a web log on the site, and had done with it. But the book would be quite a lot less … existent … shall we say? And really we couldn't have done it that way.

As Chesterton noted, sometimes you have to go all the way around the world, only to return home. They don't call Christ the Alpha and Omega for nothing, and we didn't start, and now prepare to end, this book with The God Man for nothing neither.

Look at the result of love in the life of Jesus Christ and we'll see what God wants. God loves us and gave himself for us, and now he asks us to give ourselves for him and for others. He's not loving us and then letting us go and do our thing. He loves us to possess us completely, wholly.

Sometimes we think love asks for nothing, but the truth is, it may ask for everything. We look at someone. We love them. We say, you do not need to do anything; we will love you regardless, in total surrender and sacrifice. We can make a case for that.

We can make a case for this, too: we love you, and because we do, as we're drawn to you, and we're drawn to see you become all God wants in that, you must do all.

As George MacDonald puts it: We want you to become as beautiful as he did when he thought of you first. It's a voracious all-consuming love: scripture says God is a consuming fire. The expression of his being is to love us utterly, and the expression of our being now is to do the same. It is to grow, in Christ, and God sanctifies us through life more and more, and so we learn to give more and more, and at some point it's not a duty anymore — it's an expression of who we are just as the first example of it was an expression of who he is.

We put it all together — we put the 10 Commandments here, and the Fruit of the Spirit there, and maybe the Love Chapter we like, here. We toss in some virtues, like we said in that chapter. Do all that and we'll get … like 813 different ways to start loving, and we can start now before we know the other 812. They'll come. We promise.

We arm ourselves with the Christ's mind (1 Peter 4) and live for God.

The Greatest Story Ever Told

Begins in a manger.

The Greatest Story Ever Told Begins in a Manger. It ends, well … never. Maybe it "ends" with the ground rent in twain at a crucifixion and the galaxy lit up by an ascension, and a devoted disciple blown away by a revelation. But not really it doesn't.

It doesn't end at an end — nor does it begin at a beginning.

Genesis 1 ... Matthew 1 ... John 1 ... Revelation 1 ... some of the most famous first chapters ever, all begin *in media res* — in the middle of it all and the story is already started.

- Genesis 1 — When it starts, God's already there: in the beginning, God. That is, before the beginning began to begin ... God. God God God God God. Can't get any firster than that.

- Matthew 1 — That's a genealogy, people, and a robust and hardy, and a *long* one, at that. Talk about something already having started: try three or four dozen generations.

- John 1 — Mirroring Genesis, yadda yadda ... now it's focused on the Christ and Holy Trinity! It turns out *He* was there before the beginning began to begin, too. Doncha love stories?

- Revelation 1 — Even as everyone from John to his readers thinks it's all about to wind down (we checked, and it is the last of all the books), what happens? God starts it up again with the whole 'nother thing He shows the disciple whom Jesus loved.

God is all about beginnings, and endings, too ... which turn out to be the beginnings ... which end ... which ... think of it like eternity, but no pesky math. And if it starts to fold in on itself or something, well, that's quantum physics, right? At least a tesseract.

Beginnings ... new beginnings if you insist, though that's more than a little redundant ... but you know behold He makes all things new, right?

Whenever: if we talk beginnings new or old, endings gone or coming

God.

One last thing, also first

Sometimes love is not enough.

Or at least the *wording* "Love your neighbor" isn't. It's a summation, as a lawyer. Work with us on this one a bit. We don't have to read the entire Bible every time we want to know what to do; we have a summation: we should love our neighbor.

Now that still needs to be worked out, as we've been saying this entire part two. Because *we know*: Love God ... Love Our Neighbor. But we get more complex, dig a bit deeper, to know what that *means*. We've tried to do this.

Then we come full circle and remember, remind ourselves, however it *is* worked out, the summation is ... love.

Unique to Christianity is *love* as the ethic. Everything hangs on it, said Jesus, meaning all scripture and all law and all ways we can, and should, try to meld the two, must be sayable in the summation: Love God, Love Our Neighbor.

Then we go farther.

We say Jesus *is* the summation — the essence and the exact image of the invisible God, who is love. Christian ethics at its core is Jesus Christ ... the person and work, the full monty, however you want to say it.

He's the measure of it.

He's the guy.

The law works in there (we've said this) and it's good, and it's from God. It can't save, but it's all kinds of good things. One good thing is it points to Jesus Christ.

Imitation has been called the sincerest form of flattery. If so, dozens of other faith practices flatter us no end, and quite sincerely — and really, I mean, stop it guys. We're blushing.

They flatter us because they'll crib all the love of God and neighbor off Christianity's paper. Then they offend because they pretend they didn't, and they don't take Christ. If they did, they'd have to become Christians.

Love costs, and we define it. It's not a word, or a feeling, or a thing that comes and goes. It is what we are and what we do or don't, and certainly good works and expressions of love for God and neighbor, that, again ... *we can do.*

Love is a condition of the soul that can grow by doing this. One thing it's not is some undefined *goo* for us to shape into what we want it to be.

The Bible's love chapter we all talk about is all about self-sacrifice and self-discipline and self-denial — actions that cost: patience and kindness, being neither proud nor rude, neither envious nor boastful.

And the most perfect expression of it is Jesus Christ. He lived in self-sacrifice and self-discipline and self-denial — and it ends in dying for His neighbor, which is all of us.

Go and do likewise.

What does Jesus think about love? He says there's no greater kind than to lay down one's life. What does He do about it? Same thing.

Thinking ... believing, believing ... thinking: united in Christ.

About Apologetics.com

Apologetics.com exists to remove intellectual impediments to Christian faith, enhancing believers' confidence in, and weakening skeptics' objections, to the gospel message.

We want to present a passionate, winsome Christianity — the truth it claims, the love it proclaims, and the life it offers in the Kingdom of God.

In all our apologists do, we aspire to provide first-rate Christian apologetics resources and training to the public through our website, radio broadcasts, publications, and related activities. On this, please find us through

- Our website, www.apologetics.com, to contact us directly
- KKLA-FM 99.5, in Southern California, Fridays at Midnight
- Conferences, a speakers bureau, and publications and books

If you know us, you know we're actually friendly, and like a family. Now a family doesn't always agree, and sometimes it gets a little messy — but the love is there. E-mailing us questions through the website; listening, calling, and interacting with us on the show; or requesting a speaker and attending conferences — you'll see it it's true.

Apologetics inhabits and speaks to any part of life, because all of it is God's. That means there's ways to show him in, with, and through it.

In history, philosophy, culture, languages … wherever we are, God's there first, and remains, and waits, and pursues. We're here to help.

Thank you for traveling with us, looking and laboring, working and praying, for glimpses of the Good, the True, and the Beautiful —

ultimately leading us to the Creator of all which is Good, True, and Beautiful.

And finally, grow and partner with our group by donating to our non-profit organization and sending us your feedback on all that we do.

We at Apologetics.com thank you for taking the time to journey with us on this road called life, where we look and labor for glimpses of the Good, the True, and the Beautiful – which ultimately lead us to the Creator of all that which is Good and True and Beautiful!

Contact us today. Thank you.

Yours,

Apologetics.com

Who Else Wants To Be Better Equipped To Engage Others In The Conversation For Truth?

The staff of Apologetics.com is committed to not only teaching apologetics but equipping believers to go out and engage in the conversation for Truth. That's why we're pleased to announce the launch of the **Apologetics Academy**, an extension of our ministry where you can be trained in the art and science of Christian apologetics from your own living room.

Free Gift For You!

We are providing you will an access code that will give you a 90 day membership to our **Apologetics Academy** absolutely free.

Visit us at **www.Apologetics.com** and use the following access code: **thinkandlive**

Breinigsville, PA USA
14 February 2011
255533BV00001B/2/P